DO ANIMALS HAVE SOULS?

A Pet Lover's Guide to Spirituality

RABBI RONALD ISAACS

KTAV Publishing House
Brooklyn, New York

Our beloved companions

POOCHIE

TEDDY

BLACKY

MISSY

HUMPHREY

AUFRAUF

FALLON

ZOE

LEXI

PEABO

MOOKIE

MOOSE

MABEL GRACE

Copyright © 2013 Ronald Isaacs

Do Animals Have Souls? A Pet Lover's Guide to Spirituality

Library of Congress Cataloging-in-Publication Data in progress

Hardcover ISBN 978-160280-268-1
Paperback ISBN 978-160280-269-8

All rights reserved. No part of this book may be used or reproduced in any manner whatsoever without written permission from the publisher, except in the case of brief quotations embodied in reviews and articles.

Typeset by Ariel Walden for Urim Publications

Illustrations reproduced from Vero Shaw, *The Illustrated Book of the Dog* (London, c. 1881)

Printed in USA

Published by KTAV Publishing House
527 Empire Boulevard, Brooklyn, NY 11225
Tel. 718-972-5449, www.Ktav.com

FRANKLIN TOWNSHIP PUBLIC LIBRARY
485 DEMOTT LANE
SOMERSET, NJ 08873
732-873-8700

Contents

6
————

Contents

8

Contents

Acknowledgments

I AM GRATEFUL TO THE FAMILIES OF TEMPLE Sholom for allowing me the privilege of being their rabbi. Over the years they have asked me numerous questions on a variety of subjects. Their questions about animals and their pets have served as the motivation for writing this book. My appreciation goes to my publishers Bernie Scharfstein, Tzvi Mauer, Moshe Heller, and Oscar Rijo for his graphic design work. My thanks to Holly Sher, CEO of Evanger's Dog & Cat Food Company, who introduced me to Kosher for Passover pet food. Lastly, my sincere gratitude to Laura Friedman, Executive Director of the Shimon and Sara Birnbaum JCC, who afforded me the opportunity of blessing the animals at Dog Day at the J.

I dedicate this book to all of the pets I have ever had throughout my life, especially my current best friend Lexi, a beautiful golden retriever, and my granddogs Peabo and Mookie, two very sweet pugs.

A person should feed his or her animal before eating

(Babylonian Talmud Berachot 40a)

Introduction

Sixty-two percent of all Americans own pets: 78 million dogs and 86 million cats. This is an amazing statistic. Today one can purchase pet insurance, pet bereavement cards, pet beds, pet toys, pet clothing, and pet houses. There are pet cemeteries, pet spas, pet trainers, pet babysitters, pet vacations, pet meds, and a wide variety of premium pet foods and snacks. (There is even kosher pet food!) Many of us who own pets have formed deep and powerful bonds with them. They have become faithful companions. My family and I have owned dogs almost my entire life. My first was a dog named Poochie, followed by a beagle called Teddy. In married life there were Humphrey and Aufrauf (cocker spaniels) and twenty-five years of golden retrievers: Fallon, Zoe, and now Lexi. Anyone who has ever owned a pet knows what a good friend a pet can be. Having a pet has the additional educational benefit of teaching children how to care for another creature. George Eliot once wrote that animals are such agreeable friends – they ask no questions, they pass no criticisms. I could not agree more.

Animals are part of God's creation. Many centuries ago people used to worship animals. The Egyptians believed that cats were holy and worshiped a bull called Apis. Native Americans would eat deer and other hunted game and thank the spirit of the animal for providing them with the food. The ancient Israelites sent a goat off into the wilderness in the time of the Jerusalem Temple to carry away the sins of the Jewish people. This was the original scapegoat. Birds and animals were brought to the Temple as sacrifices or gifts to God.

Since biblical times the Jewish people have been given special responsibilities toward animals. Long before there were domesticated animals and animals raised as pets, the Bible indicates its concern for the animal population. The Ten Commandments includes a law legislating kind treatment of animals: the fourth commandment, which ordains the Sabbath, mandates that ". . . the seventh day is a Sabbath unto the Lord your God: you shall not do any work, you, your son, or daughter, your male or female servant, or your cattle." Given that until the end of the nineteenth century employees in this country were often expected to work seven days a week, this three-thousand-year-old concern for animals is truly remarkable.

Rabbis of bygone years have some interesting thoughts regarding what people can learn from their animals. According to the Talmud, Rabbi Yochanan said: Even if we had not been given the Torah we still would have learned modesty from the cat, honesty from the ant, chastity from the dove and good manners from the rooster. I think that these sentiments would resonate with today's pet owners, but owning pets is "a new phenomenon" because it took a while for animals to become domesticated to the point where they could live with humans. Most of the biblical animals were used as workers, such as donkeys which were used as beasts of burden.

As a rabbi of a synagogue in suburban New Jersey, I have had the pleasure of meeting many of my congregants' pets when I visit their homes. I have learned of the joy they have brought to their family, the Hebrew names that some have been given, and I often am informed of the grief of their loss and the search for a ritual that would be comforting. I have even had the opportunity to offer some of my congregants' pets my blessing (more about this later in the book).

Over the course of my rabbinic career I have been asked numerous pet-related questions. One of the more popular ones is: "Do animals have souls?" This question is of particular interest to people because they want to know upon the loss of their pet whether you could pray for it in the same way that you would pray for a person. Can you or are you allowed to mourn for a pet using the same rituals that you would use to mourn for a loved one in your family? Can you sit *shiva* (period of seven days of mourning) for your cat or recite the Mourner's Kaddish for your dog? *Do Animals Have Souls?* is meant to serve as a guide to help provide advice and counsel to those who have pets. It is my sincere hope that my advice will also be useful and adaptable to persons of all faiths. In addition to pet questions and answers, I have also chosen to include some general information about the animal kingdom in Jewish thought and answers to all kinds of questions related to the animal kingdom.

Here's hoping that this book brings you closer to your pet and guides you to a deeper spiritual understanding of how and where Judaism and pet-owning intersect. I wish you happy reading and continued companionship.

Ron Isaacs

PART 1

I	**In the Beginning**

IN THE FIRST CHAPTER OF THE BIBLE, GOD TELLS Adam and Eve to be fertile, fill the earth and master it, and rule over the fish, the birds, and all the living things that creep on earth. The clear implication is that humans are to be in charge of all of the creatures. Because they lack free will, the Bible regards animals as being on a lower plane than human beings. And in Jewish tradition these verses are viewed as a warrant for humans to use animals for labor (such as on farms) and to benefit from animals (such as using wool shorn from sheep for clothing).

Following in chapter two, God says that it is not good for man to be alone, and proceeds to create all the wild beasts and the birds of the sky. God then brings them to Adam and charges Adam with the task of categorizing, naming, and defining all the known creatures of the world. By assigning to the first man the role of naming terrestrial creatures, God bestows human authority and dominion over them. However, the Bible will go on to put limits on the degree to which the animal kingdom can be legitimately used by human beings, putting many guidelines into place to ensure that animals will not be exploited by their human masters and that they will be treated with compassion and kindness.

The moral rules concerning the treatment of animals are based on the principle that animals are part of God's creation toward which humans bear responsibility. Laws in the Bible make it clear not only that cruelty to animals is strictly prohibited but also that mercy, kindness, and compassion to them are demanded of humans by God.

The rabbinic name for the offense of cruelty to animals is *tza'ar ba'alei chayim*, literally "compassion for the pain of living creatures." Killing an animal when it is not for legitimate human need is strictly forbidden. Torturing an animal is regarded as a criminal act. According to traditional rabbinic interpretation, people were not allowed to eat meat until after the flood in the time of Noah. Adam, God's first creation, was told: "Behold, I have given you every herb yielding seed which is upon the face of the earth, and every tree, in which is the fruit of a tree yielding seed – to you it shall be for food." (Genesis 1:29) This is clear proof that as a resident in the Garden of Eden, which represents the ideal society, Adam is limited to fruits and vegetables.

By the time of Noah, meat is permitted for eating purposes: "Every moving thing that lives shall be for you; as the green herb have I given you all. You must not eat flesh with its life blood in it." (Genesis 9:4)

One of the so-called Noahide laws (laws meant to be followed by Jews and non-Jews alike) prohibits the eating of meat taken from a live animal. Originally, God expected people to be vegetarians and not kill living creatures for their food. But this ideal became corrupted into the notion that there are no qualitative differences between humans and animals, leading some people to the conclusion that they could behave like animals. God then compromised the vegetarian ideal, permitting the eating of meat but strenuously forbidding the shedding of human blood, as a way of emphasizing the distinction between humans and animals.

Both the Bible and rabbis representing its views have attached particular emphasis to respecting the needs and feelings of animals. The holy Sabbath is described as a day when the ox and the mule may also rest, the same as humans. (Exodus 20:10) The Bible prohibits muzzling an ox when it is treading out grain. (Deuteronomy 22:10) In view of the feelings of animals, the Bible cautions: "You shall not slaughter it on the same day with its young." (Leviticus 22:28) The medieval commentator Maimonides comments on this verse and explains that the pain of the animals under such circumstances is very substantial. He further asserts that there is no difference between the suffering of people and the pain felt by animals in such a case as this.

The humanitarian motive toward the animal is readily evident in the Book of Exodus (23:5), which stipulates that an enemy's beast of burden must not be deserted but rather helped when it is seen lying under its burden. The Book of Deuteronomy presents the prohibition of plowing crops using a donkey and an ox harnessed together. (Deuteronomy 22:10) Among the rationales for such a law is that the uneven steps would cause severe discomfort to the ox and distress to the smaller donkey.

Perhaps the cruelest act that any parent can endure is to see his or her child being killed. The Nazis often delighted in murdering Jewish children in the present of their parents. There is a biblical law of mercy that prohibits treating animals in the way that people like the Nazis treated human beings. It appears in the Book of Deuteronomy (22:6) and is one of two commands in the Bible (the other being to honor one's parents) that offer a reward of long life for its performance: "If you come across a bird's nest in a tree or on the ground, and the nest has young birds or even eggs, and the mother is sitting with her young, do not take the mother together with her children. Let the mother go and take only the young – so that you may fare well and live a long life." The rabbinic commentator Nahmanides understands this religious obligation in terms of education to mercy: by not being allowed to take the offspring in the mother's presence, by practicing compassion to animals, we become even more compassionate to human beings. This religious obligation is a reminder that animals, like human beings, can suffer emotionally. Just as we cannot wantonly cause them physical pain, so we cannot add to their mental anguish. This is yet another reason why it is important for parents who see their child tormenting their dog or cat, or even willfully killing a fly and enjoying it, to stop the child firmly and impress upon him or her the laws mandating the kindness that we must afford animals. Kindness is so important with regard to the goodness of humans that the Book of Proverbs (12:10) reminds us: "A righteous person knows the soul and needs of his animal."

Animals and their young have a bond, and this idea is a good starting point for teaching our own children compassion. Above all, pet owners must constantly remind themselves that even though their pets are animals, they are living beings who have been entrusted to their care. They should be treated with utmost care and compassion, and afforded every opportunity to experience the joys of life and love that are offered to them. Long before there were Societies for the Prevention of Cruelty to Animals, these biblical laws taught the sacredness of life, the Jewish trait of compassion, and the constant reminder to treat animals with utmost love and care. How amazing it is that the fourth commandment not only requires humans to rest, but extends the requirement of rest and relaxation to one's own animals as well. Wherever one turns we see that Jewish tradition regards the life of all of God's creatures, animals included, as sacred.

II — Our Pets: The Jewish Viewpoint

I HAVE LIVED IN A HOUSE WITH A DOG EVER SINCE I was a little child. Our newest addition is a golden retriever named Lexi, and she is an integral member of the family. She celebrates Shabbat with us by lowering her head to receive her special blessing, tastes the challah, and patiently sits by our side as we sing the Grace after Meals. I am not the only American who has a family pet. According to the National Pet Owners Survey, conducted by the American Pet Products Manufacturers Association a few years ago, Americans have almost 89 million cats and 75 million dogs. Pet ownership has reached an all-time high with 71 million households owning at least one pet. Almost a quarter of all dogs have their own beds, over 40 percent of Americans share a bed with their dog, and almost half of all dog owners consider their pet's comfort when purchasing a new vehicle. Most pet owners surveyed say they consider their pet a member of the family, and three in four believe that their dogs tried to make them feel better when they were unhappy. I'm a believer, too. I also strongly feel that my life is more satisfying and less stressful due, in part, to having Lexi in my house. (In fact, she is lying next to me right now as I am writing this chapter of the book on my computer.)

In bygone years and until fairly recently, many rabbis held the view that a domesticated animal found in one's home or on one's farm had a purpose to perform some task for the household. The thought of a household pet such as a dog or cat whose raison d'être was to offer companionship to its owner was unheard of among Jews. When a household pet indeed was present in a Jewish home, it was often considered an unnecessary indulgence and a waste of time. The medieval French commentator Rashi referred to animals such as monkeys and lions which kings would possess to be a waste of time with no benefit whatsoever. Other rabbinic sources included animals such as cats and squirrels in the "waste of time" category.

These days we have a completely different attitude toward house pets, which have been shown in studies to be a source of great joy and companionship. When making my rounds, I have often seen animals brought to hospitals for the sole purpose of cheering up patients. Families with children have often spoken about how their pets have helped their children learn the value of caring and being responsible for the welfare of their creatures. Many older people who live alone have spoken about the companionship that their pet has afforded them. Furthermore, learning to care for pets can introduce children (and their parents as well) to the value of caring for others and of taking on responsibility for the welfare of other creatures. Caring for and living with household pets might also serve to inspire us with a true sense of responsibility for the animal kingdom in general.

Jews have been called "the People of the Book," but we are just as surely the "people of the family." We began centuries ago as a family with Abraham, Isaac, Jacob, Sarah, Rebekah, Rachel, Leah, and their children. Strong family ties and a proliferation of children were important Jewish values. Pet owners soon come to the realization that they have added another member to their family. Life will never quite be the same, and responsibilities will increase in complexity. But, hopefully, there will be many rewards as well.

When purchasing a pet, do not assume that all household pets for sale to the general public are raised under conditions that an ethically sensitive consumer should support or endorse. On their website, the

American Society for the Prevention of Cruelty to Animals describes the practices in place at so-called puppy mills which are often overcrowded and conditions most unsanitary. Because compassion to animals is a time-honored tradition, Jews (and others) should consider themselves forbidden to purchase any pet from businesses that treat animals unkindly. Of course, dogs, cats, and other animals are also always available from public shelters and pounds.

Taking animals into our homes as pets obligates us to ensure that they are properly cared for, including food and medical care should they need it. There is an absolute requirement according to Jewish law to make sure that our pets are properly attended to before we ourselves partake of food. Our pets must have space and opportunity for regular exercise. Additionally, we must be careful to protect our pets from being abused by young children or visitors.

Jews also have a responsibility to be good neighbors and to see that our animals do not harm or cause damage to the property of others, to other animals, or to people. The Talmud in several places (Shabbat 63a, Ketubot 41b) prohibits keeping dangerous animals in our homes. And, surely, it is our obligation to always clean up after our pets.

The longer one has a loving pet, the more attached one becomes. If such a pet develops a life-threatening illness, one must decide whether putting it to sleep is a "kosher" Jewish option. Here guidance from one's pet doctor and rabbi would surely be useful. When a beloved pet dies the loss can be immense. There are often questions about rites of mourning for Jewish pet owners and which prayers might be appropriate when mourning one's loss. In all, the experience of owning and raising a pet can provide deep spiritual lessons as well. The great nineteenth century rabbi, Elyah Lopian, is said to have kept a cat and to have insisted on feeding it personally as a means of emulating God's constant concern for all of God's creatures.

Part II of *Do Animals Have Souls?* will present my answers to questions related to pets and queries related to animals in general. For Jews, asking questions is a national pastime. Even our holiest books are filled with questions. The great sages of Jewish tradition ask every conceivable question about every conceivable topic. Children too love to ask questions. I know, because I have been fortunate to serve as rabbi of a synagogue that abounds in children. Each year I am invited to our religious school to answer the questions of students on a variety of topics. I also have "Ask the Rabbi" sessions for adults. I have collected hundreds of questions over the years posed to me by both younger students as well as adults. The questions and answers in this book are some of the most interesting ones that have been asked over the past three decades that relate to animals and pets.

I am old enough now, and wise enough, I hope, to realize that I don't have all the answers, and to realize that the responses in this book may serve both to guide and inspire you to seek further and come up with your own answers.

The medieval poet Solomon ibn Gabirol once taught that the finest quality of a human being is to ask a question. I hope that some of these questions will resonate with you because they are your questions, too, and that my answers will help provide and guide you to the way in which Jews raise, treat, love, and even mourn their most precious pets.

Finally, our sages of bygone days remind us that while we human beings like to think of ourselves as the pinnacle of creation because humans were the last creatures that God created on the sixth day, we should remain humble and remember that the creation of even the smallest animals preceded the creation of humankind and that we are all God's fellow creatures and each has a God-given part to play in the universe. The Talmud reminds us that in the event of human arrogance, one can reply, "A mosquito took precedence over you." (Talmud, Sanhedrin 38)

Perek Shirah: **A Chapter of Song**

"*PEREK SHIRAH*: CHAPTER OF SONG" IS ONE OF the most unusual and unique books in all of Jewish literature. Scholars posit that it is one of the oldest texts of Merkavah mysticism, the first flowering Jewish mysticism in the early centuries of the Common Era. First mentioned in a polemical work of Salmon ben Jeroham, a tenth century Jerusalemite, its use in Jewish liturgy was revived in the sixteenth century in the holy mystical city of Safed, where it began to be recited as a prayer.

Perek Shirah is essentially a collection of sayings in praise of God as the creator of the world. What makes the book so unusual is that the sayings in praise of God have been placed in the mouths of God's creatures. All creation – except humans– is represented, the natural and the supernatural orders, inanimate nature, the heavens and their hosts, the planetary world, and the kingdom of animals, each according to its own kind. Together, the hymns comprise a kind of cosmic song of praise sung by the whole of creation. Most of the hymns are biblical verses, the greater part of them citations from the Book of Psalms.

At the outset it may seem strange that animals sing praises to God. However, in looking at the issue more carefully, it is apparent that the idea of animal praise is well rooted in the Bible and in rabbinic tradition. Beginning with the Bible, we read in Psalm 104:21: "The young lions roar after their prey and seek their food from God." Here we clearly learn from the Psalmist that animals petition God to provide them with sustenance and that their song of praise expresses itself in the huge roar that emerges from their mouths. This is biblical proof that animals can pray!

The prayerbook features Psalm 150 in the daily service, whose last verse is: "Let everything that has breath praise God." The ancient sages comment that this verse is intended to be understood that "for every breath that one takes, one must praise God." (Deuteronomy Rabbah 5:2, Tanchuma, chapter 9) Since animals also breathe, it thus follows that praising God must also apply to the animal kingdom.

Here are excerpts from *Perek Shirah* that specifically relate to animals that will help you better understand the nature of the book.

The Preface

By the beasts of the earth and the birds of the sky, God makes us wise. (Job 35:11)

Rabbi Yochanan said: "Even if we had not been given the Torah we still would have learned modesty from the cat, honesty from the ant, chastity from the dove, and good manners from the rooster." (Talmud Eruvin 100b)

Our rabbis tell this story: "At the time that King David completed the Book of Psalms, he became full of pride and said to the Holy Blessed One, 'Surely there is no creature which you have made that can sing songs and praises greater than mine.' At that exact moment a frog appeared before him and said, 'David, do not be so proud, for I can sing songs and praises even more magnificent than yours. And not only that, but in every song that I sing there exist three thousand allegories. For it is said: "God composed three thousand proverbs, and His songs numbered one thousand and five."'" (First Kings 5:12)

The Songs

The rooster says: "At the time that the Holy Blessed One comes among the righteous ones who dwell in the Garden of Eden, all the trees of the Garden pour out fragrant spices and sing and offer praises. Then he too is aroused and offers praises."

The rooster crows in seven voices:

The first voice says: "Lift up your heads, O you gates, and be lifted up, you everlasting doors; and the Ruler of Glory shall come in. Who is this Ruler of Glory? God strong and mighty, God, mighty in battle." (Psalm 24:7)

The second voice says: "Lift up your heads, O you gates, and lift them up, you everlasting doors, that the Ruler of Glory may enter. Who is this Ruler of Glory? God of Hosts, God is the Ruler of Glory. Selah." (Psalm 24:9)

The third voice says: "Arise, righteous ones, and busy yourselves with Torah so that the reward will be doubled in the World to Come."

The fourth voice says: "I wait for your salvation, O God." (Genesis 49:18)

The fifth voice says: "How long will you sleep, lazy one?" (Proverbs 6:9)

The sixth voice says: "Do not sleep lest you come to poverty; open your eyes and you shall be satisfied with bread." (Proverbs 20:13)

The seventh voice says: "It is time to act for God: they have violated your Torah." (Psalm 119:126)

The chicken says: "God gives food to all flesh. God's steadfast love endures forever." (Psalm 136:25)

The dove says: "I piped like a swift or a crane, I moaned like a dove . . ." The dove speaks before the Holy Blessed One, "Sovereign of the Universe, may my food be as bitter as the olive but entrusted to Your hand rather than sweet as honey and dependent on one of flesh and blood." (Talmud Eruvin 186)

Perek Shirah: A Chapter of Song

The eagle says: "You, God of Hosts, God of Israel, bestir yourself to bring all nations to account. Have no pity on all the treacherous villains." (Psalm 59:6)

The crane says: "Praise God with the lyre, with the ten-stringed harp sing to God." (Psalm 33:2)

The sparrow says: "Even the sparrow has found a home, and the swallow a nest for herself in which to set her young, near your altar, O God of Hosts, my Ruler, my God." (Psalm 84:4)

The swallow says: "That my whole being might sing hymns to you unceasingly; O God, I will praise You forever." (Psalm 30:13)

The peacock says: "My help is from God who made heaven and earth." (Psalm 121:2)

The desert bird says: "Light is sown for the righteous and gladness for the upright in heart." (Psalm 97:11)

The dove says: "Comfort, O comfort my people, says your God." (Isaiah 40:1)

The stork says: "Speak gently to Jerusalem, and declare to her that her term of service is over, that her transgression is expiated. She has received at God's hand double for her sins." (Isaiah 40:2)

The raven says: "Who provides for the raven his provision when his young ones cry to God?" (Job 38:41)

The starling says: "Their offspring shall be known among the nations, their descendants in the midst of the peoples. All who see them shall recognize that they are a stock that God has blessed." (Isaiah 61:9)

The domestic goose says: "Praise God. Call on God's name and proclaim God's deeds among the nations. Sing praises to God and speak of all God's wondrous acts." (Psalm 105:1-2)

The desert goose, when he sees Israel engaged with Torah, says: "A voice rings out: 'Clear in the desert a road for God. Level in the wilderness a highway for our God.'" (Isaiah 40:3)

The chicken says: 'Trust in God forever, for God is an everlasting rock." (Isaiah 26:4)

The vulture says: "I will whistle to them and gather them, for

I will redeem them. They shall increase and continue increasing."
(Zechariah 10:8)

The butterfly says: "I will lift up my eyes to the mountains for what is the source of my help?" (Psalm 121:1)

The locust says: "O God, I will extol you, I will praise Your name. For You have done wonderful things, counsels of steadfast faithfulness." (Isaiah 25:1)

The spider says: "Praise God with resounding cymbals, praise God with clanging symbols." (Psalm 150:5)

The fly, when Israel is not engaged with Torah, says: "A voice rings out: 'Proclaim.' Another asks: 'What shall I proclaim? All flesh is grass, all its goodness like the flower of the field.'" (Isaiah 40:6) "'Grass withers, flowers fade, but the word of our God shall endure forever.'" (Isaiah 40:8)

The sea monsters say: "Praise God, O you who are on earth, all sea monsters and ocean depths." (Psalm 148:7)

Leviathan says: "Praise God, for God is good, God's steadfast love is eternal." (Psalm 136:1)

The fish say: "The voice of God is on the waters, the God of glory thunders, God is upon the mighty waters." (Psalm 29:3)

The frog says: "Blessed be God's majestic glory forever and ever." (second line of Shema prayer)

The small cow who is ritually pure says: "Who is like You, O God, among the gods? Who is like You, glorious in holiness, fearful in praises, doing wonders?" (Exodus 15:11)

The large cow who is ritually pure says: "Sing joyously to God, our strength; raise a shout to the God of Jacob." (Psalm 81:2)

The camel says: "God roars from on high, God makes His voice heard from His dwelling. God roars aloud over His earthly abode." (Jeremiah 25:30)

The horse says: "As the eyes of slaves follow their master's hands, as the eyes of a slave girl follow the hand of her mistress, so our eyes are toward our God, awaiting God's favor." (Psalm 123:2)

Perek Shirah: A Chapter of Song

The mule says: "All the kings of the earth shall praise you, O God, for they have heard the words that You spoke." (Psalm 138:4)

The donkey says: "Yours, O God, is the greatness and the power and the glory and the victory and the majesty; for all that is in heaven and on earth is Yours, O God. Yours is the kingdom and you are exalted as head above all." (First Chronicles, 29:11)

The bull says: "Then Moses and the Israelites sang this song to God. They said: 'I will sing to God, for God has triumphed gloriously, horse and driver has God hurled into the sea.'" (Exodus 15:11)

The animals of the field say: "Blessed be God who is good and does good." (Blessing upon hearing good news)

The deer says: "And I will sing of Your strength, extol each morning Your faithfulness. For you have been my haven, a refuge in time of distress." (Psalm 59:17)

The elephant says: "How great are Your works O God, how very deep are Your thoughts." (Psalm 92:6)

The lion says: "God goes forth like a warrior, like a fighter God whips up His rage. God yells, God roars aloud, God charges on His enemies." (Isaiah 42:13)

The bear says: "Let the desert and its towns cry aloud, the villages where Kedar dwells. Let Sela's inhabitants shout, call out from the peaks of the mountains. Let them do honor to God, and tell God's glory in the coastlands." (Isaiah 42:11-12)

The wolf says: "In all charges of misappropriation, pertaining to an ox, a donkey, a sheep, a garment, or any other loss, whereof one party alleges, 'This is it' – the case of both parties shall come before God. The one whom God declares guilty shall pay double to the other." (Exodus 22:8)

The fox says: "Woe to the one who builds his house by unrighteousness, his chambers by injustice, who uses his neighbor's service without pay and does not give him his wages." (Jeremiah 22:13)

The cat says: "I pursued my enemies and overtook them. I did not turn back till I destroyed them." (Psalm 18:38)

The insects say: "Let Israel rejoice in its Maker, let the children of Zion exult in their King." (Psalm 149:2)

The serpent says: "God supports all who stumble, and makes all who are bent down stand up straight." (Psalm 145:14)

The scorpion says: "God is good to all, and God's mercy is upon all God's works." (Psalm 145:9)

The snail says: "Like a snail that melts away as it moves, like a woman's stillbirth, may they never see the sun." (Psalm 58:9)

The ant says: "Go to the ant, you sluggard. Consider her ways and be wise." (Proverbs 6:6)

The mouse says: "And you are righteous about all that befalls us, for you act in truth and we have done evil." (Nehemiah 9:33)

The rat says: "Let everything that has breath praise God, Hallelujah." (Psalm 150:6)

The dogs say: "Come, let us bow down and kneel, bend the knee before God our Maker." (Psalm 95:6)

Blessed be God, the God of Israel, who alone does wonders. And blessed be God's glorious Name forever. May God's glory fill the entire earth. Amen and Amen.

THERE ARE SOME ONE HUNDRED AND TWENTY names of animals in the Bible, representing mammals, birds, and reptiles. There is more of a scarcity of animal names in Talmudic literature because Jewish law mentions them in the main only for the Jewish dietary laws and the laws of kosher slaughtering. This chapter presents a variety of quotations culled from many different sources that will help shed light on the importance of animals in Jewish tradition.

A righteous person takes heed for the life of his beast. (Proverbs 12:10)

A person should not eat before he feeds his own animal.
(Talmud, Berachot 40a)

It is a good sign for a person when his animal eats and is satisfied. (Sifre)

Mountains leap like rams, and hills like lambs. 　　(Psalm 114:5, recited as part of the Hallel psalms of praise on Jewish festivals)

Praise God, O you who are on earth, all sea monsters and ocean depths.
(Psalm 148:7)

According to the Talmud (Berachot 58b), our Rabbis have taught that one who beholds an elephant or an ape says: "Blessed be You, God, who varies the forms of Your creatures."

Animal Omen: One who wishes to engage in business and wants to ascertain whether he will succeed or not should rear a cock. If he grows plump and handsome, he will succeed.   (Talmud Horayot 12a)

Animal Omen: Our masters taught: when dogs howl, the angel of death has come to the city. When dogs frolic, the Prophet Elijah has come to the city. This is so, however, only where there is no bitch among the dogs.   (Talmud Baba Kamma 60b)

Animal Omen: There are three sayings in connection with an ox in a dream. If one dreams that he eats his flesh, he will become rich. If that an ox has gored him, he will have sons that will contend together in the study of Torah. If that an ox bit him, sufferings will come upon him.   (Talmud Berachot 57a)

Where there is no forest, there can be no bears.   (Talmud Sotah 47a)

You can't put the cat in charge of the cream.   (Yiddish folk saying)

If the Law had not been given to us, we might have learned chastity from the cat.   (Talmud Eruvin 100)

Gazelles are the animals most loved by God . . . because a gazelle harms no one, and never disturbs the peace.   (Midrash Samuel 9)

If you throw a bone to a dog, he will lick even the dust on your feet.
          (Zohar)

Animal Quotes and Sayings

It is not the mouse that is the thief, it is the hole . . . if there were no mouse how should the hole come by it? (Talmud, Gittin 45a)

If a man drinks properly he becomes strong as a lion, whom nothing in the world can withstand. When he drinks to excess, he becomes like a pig that wallows in mire. (Tanchuma Noah 13.21b)

When the shepherd is on the right path, the sheep too are on the right path. (Pirke de Rabbi Eliezer)

Poverty is becoming to a daughter of Jacob as a red strap to a white horse. (Song of Songs Rabbah 1:24)

Egypt is like a fair heifer. (Jeremiah 46:20)

Be a tail to lions and not a head to foxes. (Ethics of the Fathers 4:20)

Dogs in a kennel snarl at each other, but when a wolf comes along they become allies. (Talmud, Sanhedrin 105a)

As the camel, so is the burden. (Talmud Sotah 13b)

And in that day I will make a covenant for them with the animals of the field and with the fowl of the heaven and with the creeping things of the ground. (Hosea 2:20)

> All go to one place, all are of the dust.
> Who knows the spirit of men whether it goes upward;
> And the spirit of the animal whether it goes
> downward to the earth? (Ecclesiastes 3:19-21)

I will give grass in your fields for your cattle, and you shall eat and be satisfied. (Deuteronomy 11:15)

DO ANIMALS HAVE SOULS?

You shall not plow with an ox and an ass together.

(Deuteronomy 22:10)

Remember the Sabbath day, to keep it holy. Six days shall you labor and do all your work, but the seventh day is a Sabbath unto God; in it you shall do no manner of work, not you, nor your son, nor your daughter, nor your man-servant, nor your maidservant, nor your cattle, nor the stranger that is within your gates.　　(Exodus 20:8-10)

Do not boil a kid in its mother's milk.　　　　　(Exodus 23:19)

If you see the ass of him who hates you fallen due to its burden, you shall surely not pass him by; you shall surely unload it with him.

(Exodus 23:5)

It is customary to say to one who puts on a new garment: "May you wear it out and acquire a new one." But we do not express this wish to one who puts on new shoes or a new garment made of fur or leather . . . because a garment like this requires the killing of a living creature, and it is written: "And God's mercy is upon all His works." [Psalm 145:9]　　　　　　　　　　　　　Code of Jewish Law.

Praised are You, Adonai our God, Ruler of the Universe, who has given the rooster intelligence to distinguish between day and night.

(First blessing of the morning in the Jewish prayerbook)

If you come across a bird's nest in a tree or on the ground, and the nest has young birds or even eggs, and the mother is sitting with her young, do not take the mother together with her children. Let the mother go and take only the young—so that you may fare well and live a long life.　　　　　　　　　　　　　　　(Deuteronomy 22:6)

If an animal falls into a ditch on the Sabbath, place pillows and bedding under it [since it cannot be moved until the end of the Sabbath]

(Talmud, Shabbat 128b)

When an ox, sheep, or goat is born, it should stay with its mother for seven days. From the eighth day on, it is acceptable as an offering by fire to God. However, no animal from the herd or flock can be slaughtered on the same day with its young. (Exodus 22:30)

When animals lose their young, they suffer great pain. There is no difference between human pain and the pain of other living creatures.

(Guide for the Perplexed III:48)

The wolf shall dwell with the lamb, the leopard shall lie down with the kid. The calf, the young lion, and the fat ox together . . .

(Isaiah 11:6-7)

DO ANIMALS HAVE SOULS?

V   Animal Tzedakah Organizations

IN THE UNITED STATES ALONE IT IS ESTIMATED that some three to four million pets are euthanized each year, and millions of dogs and cats are strays that are left without a home or people to care for them. Natural disasters, such as what we witnessed in New Orleans with Hurricane Katrina, also put many thousands of pets at risk of losing their caring homes. There are many charitable organizations that focus on how animals can help heal people. Among these are service animals that help the sick or disabled or sanctuaries where children can learn the responsibility that comes from caring for an animal.

There are over one million different animal species on earth and only 50,000 nonprofits to help them. Some help people adopt stray animals as pets and rescue those that are at risk or abandoned. Some run low-cost spay and neuter programs or help owners with high veterinarian bills. Others fight for animal rights and still others fight against extinction by protecting endangered species. Here are some nonprofits for you to consider that have a proven record of competence and effectiveness.

1. ASPCA (American Society for the Prevention of Cruelty to Animals): The ASPCA is a nationwide non-profit organization, the oldest humane

society in North America, and still one of the largest. Its mission as an animal charity is to prevent animal cruelty. It also boasts of community outreach and adoption programs, and provides animal health services. In addition, it offers grants to animal welfare organizations and agencies across the country to aid them in their individual efforts. To learn more, visit aspca.org

2. Dogs for the Deaf: This dog charity places dogs in the houses of hearing impaired and special needs people. Rescued from animal shelters in the Oregon, California, Washington, and Idaho areas, these dogs receive medical treatment and microchips, and then are professionally trained to assist those in need. Dogs for the Deaf's programs also include: Autism Assistance Dogs for children and families living with autism; Miracle Mutts for those with anxiety, post-traumatic stress disorder, depression and more; and Program Assistance Dogs that aid those who work with the disabled or challenged. To learn more, go to: dogsforthedeaf.org

3. Foster Parrots, Ltd: This pet charity is dedicated to rescuing and providing sanctuary for unwanted, abused, or neglected parrots. In May 2008 it opened The New England Exotic Wildlife Sanctuary in Hope Valley, Rhode Island, where they are able to provide permanent housing for unadoptable parrots and other exotic animals.

4. Too Many Bunnies: This Los Angeles, California based pet charity and rescue group works with both individuals and animal shelters to find loving homes for domestic rabbits that have been abused, abandoned, or neglected. Housed in foster homes, these rabbits are rehabilitated and receive veterinary care before being put up for adoption. This pet charity also strives to educate people about rabbits and their needs, and even allows families to borrow a bunny to see if he or she will be a good fit before adoption. Go to toomanybunnies.com for more information.

5. Guide Dogs of America: Its mission is to provide the blind and visually impaired with a guide dog and companion to increase their independence and mobility. Guide Dogs of America breeds their own dogs – a mix of 70% Labrador retriever, 15% golden retriever and 15% German shepherd. They are cared for by foster families until they reach 18 months. The dogs then enter the Guide Dog Program. Go to guidedogsofamerica.org for more information.

6. The Pets for the Elderly Foundation: By supporting this charity, you can give a senior citizen a new lease on life. By partnering with 58 shelters in 30 states to cover the costs of adopting a pet, the Pets for the Elderly Foundation helped match 6,500 animals with people over the age of 60. Go to petsfortheelderly.com for more information.

7. HALO Animal Rescue: HALO stands for Helping Animals Live On. It is a no-kill pet charity that houses animals most in need. Rather than accept animals from the public, HALO gives dogs and cats that are about to be euthanized at open admission shelters a second chance by providing them with a temporary home at their adoption center facility in Phoenix. Since 1994, it has adopted more than 20,000 animals. For more information go to halorescue.org

8. PetSmart Charities: This independent wide-reaching pet charity partners with over 2,000 animal welfare organizations across the United States to create and support programs that save the lives of pets. PetSmart Charities has Adoption Centers located in PetSmart stores and often hosts fundraisers like PetWalk, a festival and a 5K walk to celebrate pets. Visit petsmartcharities.org for more information.

9. Millan Foundation: Founded in 2000 by Dog Whisperer Cesar Millan, this foundation's primary goal is to provide financial aid and educational materials to non-profit shelters across the country in order to assist in the rehabilitation and re-homing of shelter dogs. The Millan

Foundation also gives grants to non-profit shelters to spay and neuter animals in order to keep the animal population under control. Go to millanfoundation.org for more information.

10. Israel Guide Dog Center for the Blind: This organization works to improve the quality of life of blind people by providing them with safe mobility, independence, and self-confidence through the faithful assistance of guide dogs. Go to israelguidedogs.com for more information.

11. INTRA: The Israel National Therapeutic Riding Association: This organization helps people with disabilities by providing special horses for therapeutic horseback riding. Disabilities include cerebral palsy, multiple sclerosis, head injuries as well as learning and emotional disabilities. Go to NARHA.org for more information.

12. Heifer International: This global non-profit organization gives animal gifts such as cattle, sheep, rabbits, chicks, goats, geese and other regionally appropriate livestock to help communities become self sustaining and end their hunger. Go to Heifer.org for more information.

PART 2

PART 2

General Questions

I. *Why do I hardly ever see Orthodox Jews with dogs, cats, or any other pets?*

I've actually done some research into this one and there is no single answer to your question. I'm not sure what interaction you have had with Orthodox Jews, and you need to know that there are many different brands of Orthodox Judaism, some more modern and some much more traditional (wearing their special black clothing and hats). Unless you have been inside the homes of many religious Jews, you probably would not really know if there was a cat or a bird or even a rabbit that is a part of their household.

Dogs are the most public of pets, and many dogs would often be seen being walked outside of the house. In terms of the Torah's view of dogs, there is a reference in the book of Exodus stating that when the Israelites were leaving Egypt, "no dog wagged its tongue against the children of Israel." In other words, the dogs in the Bible are being lauded for not barking so that the Israelites could escape without bringing added attention to themselves.

The rabbis in the Talmud prohibit both the ownership of a dangerous animal and any animal that is even perceived as dangerous, even if in reality it is not. Here we see the sages' concern for the potential emotional distress that an animal could cause, even if that animal were not dangerous but merely perceived as such.

There is, in addition, a history of dogs being used to frighten and intimidate Jews, first in the pogroms and later in the period of the Holocaust. It is possible, therefore, that fear of dogs could pass from generation to generation, even if the fear is unwarranted. The ultra-Orthodox and people who are the closest to the old country may fall into this category. It is also a known fact that pet ownership increases in households consisting of a married couple without children, who use the pet as a sort of trial and practice run to having kids. My own daughter and son-in-law fall into this category, purchasing a pug before having their first child. Other households of persons living alone or with grown-up children may also choose to have a pet for its companion and loyalty. I know many in my own community that fall into this category. Since married Orthodox Jews generally have larger families, there may be less incentive to add a pet to the mix of many children.

So I don't think you can say that Orthodox Jews in general do not own pets, because I've been to Orthodox communities and seen modern Orthodox Jews who are on the street with their dogs. But in Orthodox circles the practice run for having children is usually having children, not pets!

2. *Are there any unusual or noteworthy animals that are particular to Jewish tradition that you can tell me about?*

References to the animal kingdom pervade biblical, Talmudic, and midrashic Jewish writings. Scores of animal species, including domestic and wild animals, insects, fish, and birds appear throughout these texts. Many metaphorical and allegorical allusions to animals are also found in different literary forms among Jewish writings. In legendary literature alone, there are thirty-six Hebrew and Aramaic animal tales designated as fox fables. There is even a conception that each species of animal sings its own particular hymn of glory to its Creator, as in the work *Perek Shirah* described in Part One of this book.

There are several noteworthy animals that have always impressed me. One is the serpent in the Book of Genesis (chapter 3) who has legs and the ability to talk. The role of the serpent is to convince Adam and Eve to eat from the forbidden tree, and as a result man and woman discover intellectual and ethical knowledge and the snake is punished by losing its legs and spending the rest of its life crawling on its belly. The association of serpents with guile is an old one, and Mesopotamian texts portray serpents as opposing the will of the gods. There are even post-biblical texts that identify the serpent of Eden with Satan himself.

Snakes also play an important role in two incidents in Israel's history: Rods are turned into serpents by Moses and the Egyptian magicians (Exodus 4:3; 7:9-15) and serpents are agents of a plague in the wilderness. (Numbers 21:6-9)

In rabbinic literature, the ram that Abraham sacrificed instead of Isaac (Genesis 22) was said to have been created on the twilight of the first Sabbath. Its ashes were said to comprise the foundation of the future Temple altar while its horn was destined to be sounded atop Mount Sinai during the revelatory experience. (Pirke de Rabbi Eliezer 31)

Balaam's donkey (Book of Numbers 22, 23) was gifted with the power of speech, and according to the Ethics of the Fathers was created for this later role on the sixth day of creation. This amazing tale, as in so many tales in folklore when animals behave like humans, raises the questions of what it means to be human and what makes us different from other animals.

Noah's dove was depicted in rabbinic literature as actually being able to talk to God as she declares: "May my food be as bitter as the olive but entrusted to Your hand rather than be sweet as honey and dependent on a human." (Talmud Eruvin 18b)

Jonah was swallowed by a big fish large enough to allow him to survive inside for three days. And a unique one-horned creature known as a *tachash* was brought into existence so that its skin could be used as the material for the tabernacle erected in the wilderness. (Talmud Shabbat 28b)

We are told that the golden calf that was fashioned by the Israelites could actually move about at will, as if alive (Tanchuma, Ki Tissa 19:24), and King Solomon was reportedly transported to distant lands by a giant eagle (Ecclesiastes Rabbah 2:25). He also rode a large sea turtle at his coronation.

Sifre Shemini 6 describes a creature called the *adneh hasadeh*, a plant-man with leaves sprouting forth from his head. The Tosafot commentary to Bechorot 1:1 describes dolphins that are half human and half fish. And the Talmud (Eruvin 18a) describes the first man as sporting the tail of an animal.

One of the most unusual animals in the Bible is the red heifer, a cow completely uniform in color, with no specks of white or black or without even two black or white hairs. This is extremely rare, to say the least. In the strange ritual of the red cow (Numbers 19) that defies rational explanation, the ashes of a red heifer (mixed with cedar wood, hyssop, and crimson stuff) is used to purify one who has come into contact with a dead person. The story of the red heifer is read on one of the special Sabbaths that precede the festival of Passover, referred to as *Shabbat Parah* – the Sabbath of the Cow. It commemorates the practices of purification that were observed by the Jewish people in ancient days and the preparation involved weeks before the celebration of Passover that is necessary to prepare one's own home for Passover.

3. *Are there any Jewish proverbs that relate to animals?*

Here are some proverbs that I think you will find most interesting relating to a variety of animals.

Ant: Go to the ant, you sluggard, consider her ways and be wise.
(Proverbs 6:6)

Ass: A whip for the ass, a bridle for the ass. (Proverbs 26:3)

Bear: When there is no forest there can be no bears.
(Talmud Sotah 47a)

Bee: As the bee gathers for its owner, so Israelites amass merits and good deeds for the glory of the Father in Heaven.

(Deuteronomy Rabbah 1)

Bird: Better one bird in your cage than a hundred on the wing.

(Ecclesiastes Rabbah 4)

Camel: As the camel, so the load. (Talmud Ketubot 67)

Cat: You don't put the cat in charge of the cream.

(Yiddish folk saying)

Dog: As a dog that returns to its vomit, so is a fool that repeats its folly.

(Proverbs 26:11)

Eagle: The king of birds is the eagle. (Talmud Hagigah 13)

Elephant: The elephant is frightened of the gnat.

(Talmud Shabbat 77)

Fish: The big fish in the sea gobble up the little ones.

(Talmud Avodah Zarah 4a)

Fly: The evil inclination resembles the fly. (Talmud Berachot 61a)

Fox: A fox does not die from the dust of its den.

(Talmud Ketubot 71b)

Goat: The kids you have left behind have grown to be goats.

(Talmud Berachot 63a)

Horse: Drive your horse with oats, not with a whip.

(Yiddish folk proverb)

General Questions

Lion: Can a lion become a dog? (Midrash, Ruth Rabbah 3)

Monkey: Compared with Sarah, all other people are like a monkey to a human being. (Talmud Baba Batra 58a)

48

Mouse: The cheese and the mouse, which pays the call on the other? (Yalkut Kohelet)

Ox: The ox knows its owner and the donkey its master's crib. (Isaiah 1:3)

Pig: If a man drinks properly he becomes strong as a lion, whom nothing in the world can withstand. When he drinks to excess, he becomes like a pig that wallows in mud. (Tanchuma Noah 13:21b)

Sheep: If no vineyard, why a fence. If no sheep, why a shepherd. (Mechilta Exodus 12:1)

Snake: No one can live with a serpent in the same basket. (Talmud Ketubot 72a)

Wolf: In the world to come, the wolf will spin silk and the dog will open gates. (Midrash, Ecclesiastes Rabbah 1)

Worm: Even the moon has no brightness, and the stars are not pure in His sight. How much less man, that is a worm, and the son of man, that is a maggot. (Job 25:6)

4. *Can you give some Hebrew names that are derived from animals?*

There are many human personal names that are linked to animals. Here are some of them that come to my mind:

Rachel (ewe)	Zibia (gazelle)
Hamor (donkey)	Jonah (dove)
Tola (worm)	Aryeh (lion)
Tzipporah (bird)	Ze'ev (wolf)
Gazez (one who shears sheep)	Dov (bear)
Shual (fox)	Deborah (bee)
Eglon (calf)	Chaya (living being)
Ya'el (mountain goat)	Ayalah (hind)
Orev (raven)	Tzvee (deer)

5. Does Judaism have any mythical animals in its tradition?

Indeed there are some fantastic animals that inhabit the world of myth and imagination in Jewish legend and folklore. Although you will not find any of these animals in your local zoo, these mythical animals continue to "pop up" in Jewish lore and story. Here is a who's who of the most famous of the legendary monsters:

Behemoth: Behemoth (Job 40:15-24) was a land monster, sometimes considered to be the mate of the more well-known sea monster Leviathan. It is depicted in the Book of Job as an animal that eats grass like an ox, is all muscles and strength, lives in the shady marsh, eats massive amounts of food, and can swallow the waters of the Jordan. In the light of the description of the others animals in these chapters, it would seem that the reference is to an existing animal, to which legendary details were later added.

According to the Book of Psalms (50:10), Behemoth was created out of one thousand mountains, and was deprived of the power of procreation so he would not be able to overpopulate the earth.

The hippopotamus has often been identified as Behemoth because it is the largest land animal in the Middle East, weighing up to six thousand pounds. Like the hippopotamus, Behemoth is a vegetarian.

Although in a few legends it does eat animals, Job describes animals playing unconcernedly near it. Most stories agree with Job, saying that Behemoth sheltered birds and that annually at the summer solstice it reared up on its hind legs to roar a warning to wild beasts that they should not attack domestic livestock. Most of Behemoth's time was spent nibbling lotus leaves and reeds along the Nile River.

Apparently what made Behemoth a monster was its amazing size and strength. Job said it had a tail like a cedar and bones as strong as brass.

In later Jewish literature, Behemoth appears as a purely mythical creature. Legend has it that at the end of the world's existence, Behemoth will be killed and served along with his mate Leviathan at a banquet tendered for the righteous.

Barnacle-goose: This is a bird that grows on trees, affixed by its bill. Literary interest in this creature continues to exist, partly because it appears in such sources as Aristotle and Shakespeare. Much debate continues as to whether this creature is kosher. By some authorities it is permitted as a fruit and by others it is banned as a shellfish.

Dragon: The dragon was viewed as a gigantic winged crocodile. In the New Testament it is often identified with Satan, idolatry, and sin. As a creature of the sea, it appears in several places in the Book of Psalms: "You break the heads of dragons in the waters" (Psalm 74:13) and "Praise God from earth, you dragons and all deeps." (Psalm 148:7)

Leviathan: Leviathan was an immense and terrifying sea creature. Biblical scholars who have analyzed Hebrew myths have often identified Leviathan with the primeval sea monster Tiamat, known in the Babylonian creation stories. The characteristics of this monster indicate that it is related to many sea monsters that appear in the Bible. The Book of Isaiah (51:9) mentions Rahab, a huge sea dragon that God destroyed while creating the world.

Of all the sea monsters, the one mentioned most often and described in the most graphic detail is Leviathan. The likely reason is the influence of the Canaanite monster Lotan on the myths of the early Hebrews. Lotan in Canaanite texts is described as a "tortuous serpent" with seven heads. In some stories Leviathan also is multiheaded. (Psalm 74:14)

In the stories about both Lotan and Leviathan it takes a deity to destroy the monster. In the case of Lotan, it is Baal, one of the chief Canaanite gods, who crushes the animal. In the Book of Isaiah, God is the one who kills Leviathan. (27:1)

The Bible's most detailed description of Leviathan is in Job, chapter 41. Light shines from the monster's eyes, sparks and flames shoot from his mouth, and smoke pours from his nostrils as out of a seething caldron. His breath kindles coals and his heart is as firm as stone. Job notes that no person is so bold as to go fishing for Leviathan with a hook or to play with him as with a bird. He is king over all the children of pride and the symbol of evil.

Despite all of the fear of Job's Leviathan, the sea monster appears friendlier in but one place. Psalm (104:26) says that the monster plays in the sea.

Rabbi Yochanan, the source for many of the Leviathan legends, describes an elaborate banquet at which time the flesh of Leviathan will be served as the feast for the righteous, particularly pious people who refrain from attending or participating in pagan sporting events. (Talmud, Baba Batra 74a-b) One source attributes Leviathan's death to lethal combat with a second gargantuan beast, Behemoth, while another traces the animal's demise to the hand of God (Midrash, Leviticus Rabbah 13:3). In any event, Leviathan's flesh will comprise the menu for a scrumptious messianic feast.

Phoenix: The Phoenix is a fabulous bird that is mentioned in apocalyptic literature. It has been said that "its food is the manna of heaven and dew of the earth, and from its excrement the cinnamon tree grows."

(3 Bar. 6:13) Some commentators contend that the *chol* mentioned in Job 29:18 in none other than the phoenix.

Jewish legend posits that this bird lives for a thousand years. At the end of a thousand years, fire comes out of its nest and consumes it, and leaving behind of itself about the size of an egg, it reproduces limbs and lives again. Another view holds that after a thousand years "its body is consumed, its wings moult" and it renews itself. (Midrash, Genesis Rabbah 19:5)

Re'em: This creature is a giant animal whose entire population consists of only one male and one female. Each lives at the opposite end of the earth from the other, and at the end of seventy years, they find their way to one another to mate. The male dies from a bite inflicted by the female during copulation and the female undergoes a pregnancy of twelve years. Eventually her belly bursts open and out comes twins, one male and one female, who depart to opposite ends of the earth. The process begins anew.

Shamir: The shamir is a worm that was created on the twilight before the first Sabbath. Known for its amazing strength, it has the ability to penetrate the hardest diamonds or other precious stones without leaving a grain of dust. According to legend, it could engrave the metal for the breast plate of the High Priest, and because metal tools were not allowed to be used for the building of the Jerusalem Temple, the shamir was used to hew the Temple stones.

Unicorn: The chief characteristics of the biblical unicorn are its strength and its inability to be tamed. The Book of Job (39:9-12) has the longest and most graphic description of the unicorn: "Would the unicorn agree to serve you? Would he spend the night at your crib? Can you hold the unicorn by ropes to the furrow? Would he plow up the valley behind you? Would you rely on his great strength and leave your toil to him? Would you trust him to bring in the seed and gather it in from your threshing floor?" From these verses we can see that the unicorn was both untrustworthy and untrainable.

Ziz: This creature was the ruler of all of the birds. It was five hundred miles high – with its feet on the ground and its head touching the sky. Its wings were large enough to darken the sky when spread. An egg once dropped by the female Ziz crushed three hundred cedars and flooded sixty cities. The immense wingspan of this fowl was capable of eclipsing the light of the sun. (Midrash Genesis Rabbah 19:4)

Ziz's eventual fate, like that of Leviathan and Behemoth, is a culinary one. Its flesh will be eaten at a future repast for righteous people as a reward for those who abstained from eating forbidden species of fowl.

6. *Are there any guidelines for raising a Jewish child that might also be applicable to raising a pet puppy or cat?*

This is a great question. All the sages and scholars of traditional Jewish thought agree that creating a sound and healthy relationship between parents and their children is a primary goal of Jewish child-rearing. The Bible was well aware of the effects of parent-child conflict, and cites the case of the rebellious and defiant son (Deuteronomy 21) whose parents have lost all disciplinary control over him. There are pet owners who have lost all disciplinary control over their pets. The Bible also teaches that parents bear the basic responsibility for guiding their children in developing a set of values and in choosing right from wrong in all areas of life. The Book of Proverbs (1:8) states:"Listen to the instruction of your father, and forsake not the teachings of your mother." Such guidance must begin early in life and continue throughout the growing-up period. The best way to guide children is to set the example personally. Children will watch the personal behavior of their parents and the decisions that they make. Consistency and honesty are important virtues in child-rearing.

There are some wonderful guidelines and rabbinic advice regarding obligations that parents have to their children that would be applicable to raising one's pet. For example, in the Talmud (Semachot 2:6) parents are warned never to threaten children, but rather to punish them or forgive them. In training all of my dogs, I have found that using positive reinforcement has been a great way of getting my dog to learn good habits.

The Talmud (Sotah 3) says that anger in a home is like rottenness in fruit. And the Talmud (Baba Batra 21a) states that if you strike a child, strike them only with a shoelace. It is important to "keep one's cool" with both children and pets, and the use of force ought not to be used in order to teach an expected behavior. Providing ample food and nourishment for our children is also of great importance. And that is why it is so amazing that our rabbis would have mentioned centuries ago that it is religious obligation to feed one's pet before serving oneself. (Talmud Berachot 40a)

Providing proper medical treatment to children ought to be a universal requirement for all parents, especially when children are sick or in pain. The great medieval philosopher Maimonides reminds us that when animals lose their young they suffer great pain. And he goes on to say that there is no difference between human pain and the pain of living creatures. (Guide to the Perplexed III:48)

As a parent of two children, I can always remember how, when my kids were young and well before they became verbal, I began to learn their body language and also learned to interpret its meaning. Since animals cannot speak, pet owners have to learn how to read the body language of their pets (facial expressions and the like) in order to better understand what is going on in their minds and how they can be assisted if they are in fact reaching out for help. Here, paying careful attention is primary.

An interesting statement in the Talmud (Sukkah 46b) says that a parent should not promise to give a child something and then not give it, because in that way the child learns to lie. It is also important for those owning pets to be consistent in what one promises their pet. So for example, I would never say to my dog: "Here's a cookie" or "let's get your leash and go for a walk," without actually following through. It would come as a great disappointment to my golden retriever to promise one thing and not follow through on that promise. One must be consistent in one's promises. If so, one will be rewarded.

The Code of Jewish Law (Even HaEzer 71) says that a father must provide his child with appropriate clothing. Although I have never bought dog clothing for my dog, there are dog owners whose dogs have a thinner coat of fur than mine does and who must walk their dogs in order for them to relieve themselves. (I have a grassy, fenced-in backyard.) It might well be useful in such circumstances to consider a winter coat for a pet, especially in the colder wintry weather. In New York City in the winter it is common to see dogs dressed in pet clothing, and some of the clothing is quite fashionable!

It is important to remember that discipline is an essential part of effective guidance. It means an attitude of firmness and consistency. The absence of discipline is tantamount to the absence of guidance. Discipline is also the other side of the coin of love. "For he whom God loves, God admonishes." (Proverbs 3:12) Discipline should and can convey a message of love. Whether it involves a stern look, a spanking, a gentle slap on the wrist, it should carry with it the clear-cut feeling that one's child's well-being is always in mind. Discipline with pets and punishment should always be followed by a bit of love and warmth. A dog (and a child too) should not be permitted to interpret the punishment as a rejection of oneself, only as dissatisfaction with the act committed.

And last of all, self-esteem is probably the most crucial personality ingredient a person can possess. Parents must communicate love to their children in order to build up their self-esteem, and should always point out to them the things that they are doing well. Similarly, pets enjoy words of praise and encouragement, and that will often be manifested in wagging their tails or smiles on their faces.

7. *I once heard of Jewish dream interpretation (like Joseph's ability to interpret the dreams of his brothers) that involves animals. Can you tell me more?*

The Talmudic tractate of Berachot (56b-57a) presents an array of animals appearing in dreams and their interpretation. Here are twelve animal dreams and their explanation according to the ancient sages.

Bird: One who sees a bird in his dream should rise early and say, "As birds hovering, so will God protect" (Isaiah 31:5), before another sort of verse, such as "Like a sparrow wandering from its nest, so is a person that wanders from his place." (Proverbs 27:8)

Cock: One who sees a cock in his dream may expect a child. If a hen, a fine garden and joy.

Oxen: There are three sayings in connection with an ox in a dream. If one dreams that he eats of his flesh, he will become rich; if that an ox has gored him, he will have sons that will contend together in the study of Torah; if that an ox bit him, sufferings will come upon him.

Donkey: If one sees a donkey in a dream, one may hope for salvation.

White Horse: If one sees a white horse in a dream, whether walking gently or galloping, it is a good sign. If a red horse, walking gently is a good sign, galloping is a bad sign.

Camel: If one sees a camel in his dream, death has been decreed upon him by Heaven and he has been delivered from it.

Elephant: If one sees an elephant in a dream, a miracle will be wrought for him. If several elephants, wonders of wonders will be wrought for him. The elephants are a good sign if saddled, but a bad omen if not saddled.

Goat: If one sees a goat in his dream, he will have a blessed year. If several goats, several blessed years.

Goose: If one sees a goose in a dream, then he may hope for wisdom. He who dreams of being with one will be head of an academy.

Serpent: If one sees a serpent in a dream, it means that his living is assured. If it bites him, it means that it will be doubled. If he kills it, he will lose his sustenance.

Beasts: All kinds of beasts are a good sign in a dream, except the elephant, monkey, and long-tailed ape.

Birds: All kinds of birds are a good sign in a dream, except the owl, the horned owl, and the bat.

8. *Do animals appear in Jewish prayer and in the siddur?*

There are references to animals in the prayerbook. They appear in the Sabbath Musaf service, where the reference is to the ancient Sabbath offering: "And on the Sabbath day two male lambs of the first year without blemish." (Numbers 28:9-10) They also appear in the additional Musaf festival service with references to the ancient animal sacrifices that were brought to the Temple on Jewish holy days. For example, on Passover we recall this offering: "You shall present two young bullocks and one ram, and seven he-lambs the first year." (Numbers 28:19)

In addition to these two references there are a fair number of animal references in the prayerbook in various Psalms and in the Torah that have been included for liturgical use. For example, in Psalm 114:5: "Mountains leaped like rams and hills like lambs" which is recited as part of the Hallel service. Or in another, "I will sing to God, mighty in majestic triumph, horse and driver God has hurled in the sea." (Exodus 15:1, known as the Song of Moses)

There is also a wonderful liturgical response, in the form of a special blessing related to one's sense of wonder and mystery of God's creations. According to the Talmud, Berachot 58b, our rabbis have taught that "one who beholds an elephant or an ape says: 'Blessed be You who varies the forms of Your creatures.'" This blessing responds to the wonder of God's creation of diversity in the animal kingdom.

Perhaps the animal poem par excellence and most well-known is that of Chad Gadya – One Kid, a song that appears at the end of the Passover seder Haggadah. Intended for the entertainment of the children to keep them awake until the end of the seder service, the poem consists of ten stanzas written in nursery rhyme and phrased in the simplest style of Aramaic Hebrew. It was not made part of the actual Haggadah text until late in the sixteenth century, when it was included in the Prague edition of 1590. The principal idea conveyed in the Chad Gadya song is identical to Hillel's famous utterance concerning measure for measure: "Because you have drowned others, others have drowned you. And those who have drowned you shall themselves be drowned." (Ethics of the Fathers, 2:7)

Chad Gadya is usually interpreted as an allegory which describes the trials and tribulations of Israel's journey through history. In the following hypothesis, each object in the poem symbolizes one of Israel's enemies through the years. Israel (the only kid) is purchased by the father (God) for two zuzim (two tablets of the Law) and is subjected to people who supplant each other as Israel's foes: Assyria (cat), Babylon (dog), Persia (stick), Greece (fire), Rome (water), Saracens (ox), the Crusaders (slaughterer), and the Ottomans (Angel of Death). But in the end the Holy Blessed One saves the entire Jewish people. Here is a translation of the last verse of Chad Gadya:

"Then came the Holy Blessed One, and slew the Angel of Death, that killed the slaughterer, that slaughtered the ox, that drank the water, that quenched the fire, that burned the stick, that beat the dog, that bit the cat, that ate the goat, that father bought for two zuzim. One little goat, one little goat."

9. *What are some examples of animals being represented in synagogue art and decorations?*

Most of the animals that appear in Jewish art are confined to the area of the religious symbol. Thus the ark curtain that covers the Torah scrolls in synagogue sanctuaries often portrays the form of animals such as lions, gazelles, leopards, eagles, and doves. I one received a gift of a loaf of challah on Rosh Hashanah that was baked in the shape of a fish to symbolize fertility. I have been told that some people bake festival challot in the shape of birds to symbolize the Prophet Isaiah's promise that "as birds hovering, so will God defend Jerusalem." (Isaiah 31:5)

Many medieval illustrations show that pets were a familiar part of the Jewish household. I remember seeing in an Italian Haggadah from the sixteenth century a cat and a dog happily consuming the Passover leftovers under the seder table.

There are also animals pictured on the signs of the Jewish zodiac. The lamb is used for the Hebrew month of Nisan, the ox for the month of Iyar, the crab for Tammuz, the lion for Av, the scorpion for Cheshvan, the goat for Tevet, and fish for the month of Adar.

Animal depictions are also used as signs of the various tribes of Israel. For example, the lion is the symbol of the tribe of Judah, suggesting the vigor and nobility of the tribe. Issachar is described as a large-boned ass, indicating great physical power. The tribe of Dan is described as a serpent, a horned snake. This snake is small but highly venomous, and foreshadows the ability of the tribe of Dan to fight using guerilla warfare tactics. The tribe of Benjamin is depicted as a wolf, referring to the warlike character of this tribe. These depictions are beautifully portrayed on the Chagall windows of the Hadassah Hospital in Jerusalem. I have been there numerous times to marvel at their beauty.

In addition, animal decorations have been found on paper cuts traced to Syria, Iraq, and North Africa. A variety of motifs are found, such as the seven-branched menorah, the two tablets (Ten Commandments), the Star of David, and an eagle. Around them are motifs from the animal world, including lions, deer, eagles, and tigers.

10. *Is it true that there are or once were Jewish communities that were fond of carving animals on their cemetery tombstones?*

According to Shlomo Toperoff in his book *Animal Kingdom in Jewish Thought* (Jason Aronson), the headstones in the Jewish cemetery in Prague are engraved with animals. The stag represents the name Hirsch (Tzvi), a carp for Carpeler, a cock for Hahn, and a lion for Low. In the medieval period in Germany, Toperoff cites a physician that is represented on his tombstone by a lion holding a sword. In some communities in Germany, tombstones bore the figures of dragons and bears.

In excavations at Merissa near Beit Jiyrin (3rd century B.C.E.), the grave of Apolophanes, the head of the Zidonian community at Merissa, was found, and on the stucco is painted a cock, the guardian against evil spirits.

11. *Isn't the slaughtering of an animal for food considered cruelty to animals?*

I must admit that I fully empathize with your compelling questions, but humanity is not ready to accept giving up on eating meat, and we already learned this fact in the Book of Genesis. Adam, the first human that God creates, was not permitted to eat meat, only the fruit of trees and the herb yielding seed. Thus Adam, the perfect man, as an inhabitant of the Garden of Eden, which represents the perfect, ideal society, is limited to vegetables and fruits. Not until we come to the Bible story of Noah is meat permitted to be eaten.

Human consumption of meat, which means the taking of an animal life, has constantly posed a religious problem to Judaism, even when it has accepted the necessity of it. The ancient sages were well aware of the distinction between man's ideal and his real condition, regarding food. Referring to Deuteronomy 12:20 which prohibits eating the blood of an animal, they said: "The Torah teaches a lesson in moral conduct, that man shall not eat meat unless he has a special craving for it, and shall eat it only occasionally and sparingly." (Talmud, Chullin 84a) The permission to eat meat is thus seen to be a divine concession to human weakness and human need. It is as if the Torah is stating that it would prefer humans refrain from eating meat altogether. But since desires are difficult to stop, they must at least be controlled, and if meat is to be eaten, the restriction is that you have reverence for the life that you take by not eating blood.

The laws of Jewish animal slaughter are intended to avoid animal suffering, and scientific opinion corroborates that it is the most humane method of slaughtering. Great care is exercised that the knife be regularly examined before and after it is used to determine that it is perfectly smooth with no notches that might tear the flesh. The cut severs the arteries to the head of the animal, thereby stopping circulation to the head and rendering the animal unconscious of all pain. This is not true when an animal is only stunned by a blow. The ritual slaughterer that kills the animal must be both a pious and learned person. He is obliged to recite a blessing before he executes his duties, ever reminding him of the nature of his labor and that this whole process is but a divine concession. Thus he is prevented from become brutalized by the manner of his work. It is clear from the perspective of Jewish law that the animal's life be taken in an atmosphere of respect and dignity.

There is a Talmudic story (Baba Metzia 85a) in which a calf escapes the slaughterhouse and runs away to seek shelter with the rabbi. The rabbi fails to show his compassion and tells the animal to return to the slaughterhouse for the purpose for which it was created. As punishment for his insensitivity, Rabbi Judah suffered a painful illness that lasted many years, until he finally showed compassion to a litter of weasels, which he did while quoting Psalms 145:9: "God's compassion extends to all creatures." This story is intended to always remind us of the importance of being kind to all creatures, including those whose flesh we eat.

12. *Did ancient rabbis have any specific scientific knowledge about animals that they discovered and wrote about?*

There is information found in rabbinic writings related to the rabbis' careful observation of animals. A number of these observations appear quite perceptive by contemporary standards. Here are twelve animal observations made by the sages of old.

a. An unclean fish gives birth to live young, while a clean fish lays eggs. (Talmud Bechorot 7b)

b. Dolphins multiply and increase by coupling like human beings. What are dolphins? Rabbi Judah said: Humans of the sea. (Talmud Bechorot 7b)

c. Whatever animal has its male genital outside gives birth. Whatever has its male genital inside lays eggs. (Talmud Bechorot 7b)

d. All male animals copulate with their faces to the female's back, except three, which copulate face to face – fish, man and serpents. (Talmud Bechorot 7b)

e. The pig carries its young sixty days after impregnation, and its counterpart among trees is the apple. (Talmud, Bechorot 7b)

f. Cattle have a language – each species its own.

(Lekach Tov, Genesis 3:10)

g. All fish which have scales have fins.   (Mishneh Niddah 6:9)

h. The only mammal which has a cloven hoof but does not chew its
cud is the pig.   (Talmud, Chullin 59a)

i. The lifetime of a fly is less than one year.   (Talmud, Chullin 58b)

j. Snakes shed their skin periodically, and their venom loses its potency
as they age.   (Talmud, Avodah Zarah 30b)

k. Roosters are able to shatter glass by crowing into it.

(Talmud, Baba Kamma 18b)

l. The wolf, the lion, the leopard, the panther, the elephant, the tailless
ape, and the long-tailed ape carry their young for three years.

(Talmud Bechorot 8a)

13. *I was once told that there is an aquatic animal that is used to make the
blue dye for the prayer shawl fringe. Can you tell me more?*

In the Book of Numbers 15:37–39 God said to Moses: "Speak to
the children of Israel and say to them that they shall make for themselves fringes on the corners of their garments throughout their generations. And they shall place upon each fringe a thread of blue (*techelet* in
Hebrew) . . . And you shall see it and remember all the commandments
of God and you shall do them."

In ancient times, the purple and blue dyes derived from snails were
very rare and considered worth their weight in gold. These precious
dyes colored the robes of ancient kings and princes of Babylon, Egypt,
and Greece. To wear them was to be identified with royalty.

The God-given command to affix a thread of blue to the corners of one's *tallit* was likely meant to be a constant reminder of the Israelites' stature as noble children of God.

The Mediterranean coast was the center of the dying industry of the ancient world. "Tyre purple" came from the port city of Tyre in Phoenicia (now southern Lebanon). Some say that the etymology of the word "Phoenician" itself is that of the color purple.

Because of its great value, purple dyeing eventually came under imperial control. The Romans issued edicts that only royalty could wear garments colored with these dyes. The oppression apparently drove the Jewish blue dye industry underground, and later, with the Arab conquest of Israel in the seventh century, the secret of making the blue dye was essentially lost and the dyeing process obscured.

The prominent blue on a prayer shawl fringe had all but been forgotten for many years. What has remained are the various passages in the Talmud which describe the ancient source of the blue dye – a snail known as the *hilazon*. This creature's most notable features were that it had a shell, it could be found on the northern coast of Israel, and that its body was "similar to the sea." The main characteristic of the dye made from it was that its color was similar to the sky and the sea.

In the mid 1880's a French zoologist, Henri de Lacaze-Duthiers, found that three mollusks in the Mediterranean Sea produced purple-blue dyes. One of them was determined by him and others to be the source of the ancient biblical blue. In the same century Rabbi Gershon Hanoch Leiner set out on an expedition to search for the lost mollusk. He was convinced that a certain type of squid fit the description of the coveted snail, and within a couple of years, thousands of his followers were wearing blue threads on their fringes.

In 1913 the Chief Rabbi of Ireland, Isaac Herzog, wrote a doctoral dissertation on the subject of Hebrew porphyrology (the study of purple, a word he coined). He studied Rabbi Leiner's dyeing process and discovered the truth, which was that the process called for subjecting the squid to intense heat and then adding colorless iron fillings to the mixture. This produced the blue color that indeed appeared to come from the squid ink. The Rabbi had apparently been misled by an unscrupulous chemist.

Rabbi Herzog knew of the work done by Lacaze-Duthiers and realized that all the evidence pointed to the murex trunculus as the most likely source for the blue. And thus the riddle of producing a pure blue color from the snail was accidentally solved.

Today in Israel there is a nonprofit organization called *Amutat P'til Techelet*, comprised of a group who devote their entire time to obtaining the snails that produce the blue dye, extracting it, and dyeing fringes for prayer shawls. Last year when I was in Israel I visited the *P'til Techelet* Factory in Jerusalem and purchased several of the blue fringe kits. It was truly an interesting place to visit, and features a film on how the blue for the fringes is made.

Kindness to Animals

1. *Is it ever right to have a hopelessly sick pet euthanized?*

Pets have been a part of my life ever since I was a child. The longer one has a pet, the more attached one becomes. A pet is a family member and pet owners know that medical care is part and parcel of pet ownership. There are yearly vaccines, checkups, and several visits to one's veterinarian on an annual basis is the norm. I was fortunate to have my previous golden retriever in my life for almost ten years. One day I noticed that she was not eating (even her favorite food). This is not a good sign, and I immediately took her to see our pet doctor. He took some tests, and the next day told me that she had complete kidney failure, that the situation was, as he put it, hopeless, and that what was best for my dog was euthanasia. Needless to say I was devastated to learn this sad news. Killing an animal in a humane way is not considered a violation of the law that prohibits the causing of pain to an animal. In truth, whenever one's pet is suffering from a debilitating illness, constant pain, or non-stop disorientation, euthanasia may be considered the kindest way of dealing with the situation.

2. *Is it okay to put my cat in a kennel when I go away on vacation?*

There is nothing wrong with putting your cat, or dog, or any other pet in a kennel when one goes away on vacation. It is of course important that you research the kennel to be sure that it has a good reputation and that you are fully satisfied that it can care for your pet in a professional manner. Speaking to people that you trust and who entrust their pet to a particular kennel is a good way of finding the right place for your pet. There is nothing better than a recommendation from a friend or an acquaintance that is trustworthy.

There will always be some people who will choose to have a house sitter come directly to their house and care for their pets, because they are confident that having their pet stay in an environment with which they are familiar is better for their mental and physical well-being.

There is no question in my mind that when one has a loving companion and has to go away on vacation that it is human nature to be concerned about the care and welfare that will be afforded one's pet. I often feel a sense of guilt knowing that I have to put my pet in a kennel when I go away on vacation. Recently I received an open invitation from my daughter and son-in-law who said that they would gladly care for my golden retriever when my wife and I go away for vacation. They are the proud parents of two children, and we have often taken their two pugs to stay with us when they go away on vacation. There is no deal better than that, for nothing quite beats home hospitality! So on our next trip I am looking forward to having my dog and my grand-dogs have play time together. And yes, pugs and golden retrievers do very well together, and truly enjoy each other's company.

3. *Is it okay for me to watch bullfighting on television or go to a bullfight in Spain?*

The great medieval philosopher Moses Maimonides, in his Guide for the Perplexed 3:48, writes that "when animals lose their young, they suffer great pain." There is no difference, he says, between human pain and the pain of other living creatures. It is clear to me that God does not want bullfighting, because the law of the Torah forbids inflicting pain on any living creature. Bullfights often cause the animal to die a

Kindness to Animals

slow and painful death and therefore would be outlawed in the Torah, were the activity known to have existed in biblical times. Better that you find something else in Spain or on television with which to be entertained.

In addition, the rabbis strictly forbid any participation in spectacles in which animals are pitted against humans or against other animals. The Roman gladiator battles, including those that feature human warriors against animals, were considered abhorrent to the ancient rabbis. In our own time, cockfights, bullfights, dogfights and other similar activities are strictly forbidden as violations of the laws that govern the infliction of pain on animals. It would be wrong to participate in them, watch them, or in any way benefit from them. Even wagering on their outcomes would be considered a forbidden activity.

4. *Can I buy a pet if I am unsure if I or my family can sufficiently care for its needs?*

Impulse buying is quite common when buying pets in a pet store. A young family might be browsing the store with their young children who see a beautiful puppy, proceeding to ask their parents whether they could buy it for them. Before the parents know it, the dog is taken out of the crate by the salesperson and the kids are playing with it in an enclosed play area. Soon the entire family falls in love, and the rest is history. I have also seen a family in my community who learned of another family who was giving away a dog because it could no longer care for it. The one family felt empathy for the other, and before long offered to take care of it for them.

I strongly feel that it is of utmost importance that a family considering the purchase or adoption of a pet carefully think through all of the issues and responsibilities of owning an animal. (The same should go for families thinking to have children and raise a family.) Millions of dollars are spent by pet owners on food, medical care, boarding, and pet toys. Pets require your time and your willingness to give them proper food, exercise, and medical care. All of this can be expensive, and one must be certain that one has the time and the financial resources that are necessary to raise a pet and give it a healthy, nurturing environment. Keeping a pet in a small cage or confined to a tiny apartment all alone while the family is out and about may be in violation of the Jewish principle of compassion for animals. Pet ownership may be a great joy, but it comes with responsibilities as well, and if they cannot be met, owning a pet can be a big hassle. I would therefore say that if one is not certain if ready and prepared to accept the responsibilities of owning a pet, it would be advisable to wait until the time is right.

5. *Can you tell me more about the specific Jewish law that deals with compassion towards animals?*

As far back as the Bible, we find several laws which teach compassion for animals. In the story about Noah and his family in the Book of Genesis, one of the so-called Noahide laws (laws meant to be followed by Jews and non-Jews alike) prohibits the eating of meat taken from a live animal. The religious obligation of observing Sabbath rest is extended to animals as well. Wherever we turn, we see that Jewish tradition regards the life of all of God's creatures – animals included – as sacred.

The rabbis also spoke and wrote at great length about the responsibility that humans bear toward animals. At a time in history when animals were apparently treated very cruelly by other people, the rabbis taught the *mitzvah* (religious obligation) called in Hebrew *tzaar baalei chayim*, literally "prevention of cruelty to animals." They taught that people must look after their animals and pets with great care. One of the most insightful instructions in the Talmud concerning the treatment of animals is found in this profoundly simple statement, "You must not eat your own meal until you have seen to it that all of your animals have been fed." (Talmud, Berachot 40a)

Here is some of the advice of Jewish tradition regarding caring and compassion toward animals:

When an ox, sheep, or goat is born, it should stay with its mother for seven days. From the eighth day on, it is acceptable as an offering by fire to God. However, no animal from the herd or flock can be slaughtered on the same day with its young. (Leviticus 22:26-27)

Do not cook a kid in its mother's milk. (Exodus 23:19)

When you see your enemy's donkey lying under its load and would like to leave it alone, you must nevertheless help it get on its feet. (Exodus 23:5)

If you come across a bird's nest in a tree or on the ground, and the nest has young birds or even eggs, and the mother is sitting with her young, do not take the mother together with her children. Let the mother go and take only the young – so that you may fare well and live a long life. (Deuteronomy 22:6)

Do not plow with an ox and donkey together (in the same yoke) (Deuteronomy, 22:10)

If an animal falls into a ditch on the Sabbath, place pillows and bedding under it (since it cannot be moved until the end of the Sabbath). (Talmud, Shabbat 128b)

Jews must avoid plucking feathers from live geese, because it is cruel to do so. (Code of Jewish Law, Even HaEzer 5:14)

When animals lose their young they suffer great pain. There is no difference between human pain and the pain of other living creatures. (Guide for the Perplexed III:48)

One of the most beautiful of all the stories in the Bible is one that underscores how important a person's treatment of animals is in assessing character. When Abraham dispatches his trustworthy servant Eliezer to find a suitable wife for Abraham's son Isaac, he gives him no explicit guidelines other than that the woman should come from the area in which Abraham was raised. Eliezer decides that extending kindness, both to humans and animals, is the most appropriate first criterion to look for in a mate. When a woman (Rebekah) comes out to draw water when he arrives in Nahor in the evening, he has his camels kneel down by the well. Rebekah comes to the well, offering him water, and then returns to the well again and again to draw water for all his camels. Eliezer, seeing the kindness that Rebekah has shown to the camels, immediately decides that she shall become the wife for Isaac. His mission has been accomplished.

Under the rubric of the prevention of cruelty to animals, most rabbinic authorities forbid only the infliction of gratuitous or excessive pain on an animal. However, if an animal is needed for some legitimate human purpose (e.g., a horse pulling a wagon), this is permissible, since animals were created for human benefit and to serve human needs in the world. However, one must always keep in mind that when a person utilizes the labor of an animal, the animal's discomfort must be minimalized.

6. *What is a good character test as to whether someone's commitment to preventing animal suffering is admirable?*

Joseph Teleushkin, in his book *A Code of Jewish Ethics, Volume 2, Love Your Neighbor as Yourself* (p. 328), presents an outstanding character test which is intended to determine whether a person cares more about the suffering of animals in a situation where both animals and human beings are being hurt. He cites an incident with the leadership of PETA (People for the Ethical Treatment of Animals) whose organization's mission is the prevention of cruelty to animals. In early 2003,

Palestinian terrorists sent a bomb-laden donkey with the intention of destroying an Israeli bus. While the donkey was walking toward the bus the bombs exploded, killing the donkey before it was able to kill all of the people on the bus for whom the bomb was intended. Throughout the world, Jews and many others – though sorry for the death of the donkey – were relieved that a mass murder had been averted. The response of PETA was very different. Its president wrote a letter to Yasser Arafat, chairman of the PLO (Palestinian Liberation Organization), asking him but one thing: not to stop engaging in terror against humans or for that matter humans and animals, but rather only that "he leave animals out of the conflict." PETA was pleased with the letter that its president wrote to Arafat protesting the mistreatment of animals. To have written to Arafat, a known terrorist, and speak only of not using a donkey surely conveys the impression that the PETA president was only bothered with the death of the donkey, and not the mass murder of the Israelis on the bus.

1. *Is a visually impaired person allowed to bring a seeing-eye dog into a synagogue?*

A number of years ago, a colleague of mine who had some physical disabilities and difficulty walking brought her service dog to our Temple. She was seated next to me on the sanctuary stage next to her very well-behaved greyhound. I was amazed at how well-mannered this dog was, and how obedient he was to her. After the service I learned that there were some congregants (not knowing about this special animal) who were taken aback by the fact that this dog was lying down on the sanctuary floor near the Torah Ark.

Jewish law allows people to use animals for various tasks, and for their part, the ancient sages affirmed the right of humans to use animals to assist us in our labor and in our lives. Thus one is allowed to ride on a horse, to use an animal to pull a carriage, to turn a grindstone, or to perform other similar tasks. It is not generally appropriate for one to bring pets into a synagogue sanctuary; however, a service dog who helps facilitate one's walking or seeing is in a different category. Often called "mitzvah animals" in Jewish tradition, they are permitted to enter the holy space of a sanctuary because of their special role in helping people conduct and live their lives.

A so-called assistance animal that is specifically trained to help people who have disabilities would be allowed into a synagogue. These dogs help to enhance the life of a disabled person, allowing that person more quality of life.

2. *I keep kosher. Is it acceptable to feed my pet non-kosher pet food? And what am I supposed to do on Passover?*

The Jewish dietary laws are meant to pertain to people, not their animals. Generally speaking, even pets in Jewish homes that keep kosher are allowed to eat non-kosher food. In fact, the Torah says that some kinds of non-kosher meat should literally be thrown to the dogs. (Exodus 22:30) Since most pet foods are made with non-kosher meat and meat by-product, it would be prudent to keep the pet food away from your kosher utensils and dishes. For practical reasons, many families will choose to have a special set of utensils for their pet's food.

The situation on Passover, when one must remove all leaven for their home, is different. Most pet food contains ingredients that may not be used in Jewish homes on Passover, regardless of whether they are only eaten by pets. Some families make their own kosher for Passover dog or cat food, using boiled chicken, veggies, and starches like potatoes. Rabbi Avraham Danzig, an eighteenth century rabbinic authority from Vilna, permits buying regular pet food that does not contain leaven (*hametz*). He uses the principle that people would never eat dog food.

I recently learned about a company that produces Kosher for Passover pet food called Evanger's Dog and Cat Food Company. They manufacture their pet food with the endorsement of the highly authoritative Chicago Rabbinical Council. They produce high quality pet food and they have a line of products that you can find online which does not combine any meat with dairy products and is free of all leaven.

3. *Is it permissible to own a pet pig?*

Although a myth, there are many people that still believe that the rationale for the dietary laws is purely for reasons of health. In

Photo courtesy of Evanger's Food For Dogs & Cats

Leviticus we are told which animals, fowl, and fish are permitted to be eaten. The only reason given in the Torah is that God is holy, and God wants the Jewish people to be a holy people. The pig is one of the unclean animals prohibited as food. Although it has a cloven foot, it does not chew its cud. Maimonides the philosopher observed that pork contains more moisture than is necessary for human good and too much superfluous matter. Historically the pig has been described as the symbol of everything that is repulsive and was so despised by Jews that the Talmud often refused to even mention it by name. The famous commentator Rashi noted that the swine eats anything and is also given much food, giving rise to the rabbinic expression "none is richer than the pig." (Talmud, Shabbat 155b)

The question of raising pigs in the State of Israel has brought about great controversy. The religious parties in Israel fought for a national law forbidding pig breeding, but in the early years the matter was left to local authorities. There is a kibbutz in Nazareth in the Galilee that raises pigs and has a plant to produce pork sausage.

All of this being said, although it is forbidden by Jewish law to eat the meat of a pig, it is permitted to wear pigskin shoes (even in the synagogue), carry a pigskin wallet, and even bind religious books in pigskin. One could even play with a football made of real pig skin. A pig, too, is one of God's creatures, and so yes, it is permissible to have a pet pig! But you must be certain that you have the kind of outside grounds that allow for the ownership of such an animal. A pet pig in an apartment would not be a good idea. I think a dog or cat would be a much better choice.

4. *Does Judaism have anything to say about feeding a pet?*

Because Judaism believes in treating animals in a compassionate way, it would affirm the importance of feeding a pet an appropriate amount of food at an appropriate time. Speaking to one's own pet doctor for the details would be the prudent thing to do. By far the most insightful instruction in the Talmud concerning the treatment of animals is found in this profoundly simple statement, "You must not eat your own meal until you have seen to it that all of your animals have been fed." (Berachot 40a) This law makes great sense, especially for people who own pets. Imagine what it would feel like for a pet to sit and watch you eating your meal, while it was hungry. Our own children when they were young noticed how we would always give our dog food before enjoying our own meal. Here are two wonderful lessons for parents who have pets to teach to their children: an obligation to be kind to all of God's creatures and the importance of delayed gratification. So do remember this important teaching, and take the time to feed your pet before you feed yourself. If you do this your pet will do a lot less begging for **your** food. Rabbi Joe Telushkin also recommends that if you have a pet, give it an extra treat once a week, in order to make the Sabbath special for your pet as well. Ours always enjoys an extra piece of challah on Shabbat.

5. *I recently learned that the Torah prohibits the castration of male species. What's the Jewish view today on spaying one's pet?*

In Leviticus 22:24 we are told: "You shall not offer to God that which is bruised or crushed or broken or cut." The ancient sages understood this verse to refer to animals with damaged sexual organs, and deduced from the verse that not only is it forbidden to offer a sterilized animal as a sacrifice, but also that to sterilize animals in general is a biblical prohibition.

However, it is important to report that when they state the law, authorities point to the fact that the law deals only with sterilizing **male** animals. There is even an opinion that the act of sterilization does not apply to female animals because the biblical verse refers to damaging external organs. This may be the reason why the Code of Jewish Law differentiates between a male and female. Although it is forbidden to sterilize a female animal, if one does it, there is no punishment incurred. There are also rabbinic authorities that allow a non-Jew to neuter the animals, and others that allow Jewish veterinarians to spay female pets.

Another important consideration about spaying a female pet is the Jewish law against cruelty to animals. Animal activists agree that cats and dogs should be sterilized for their own well-being, reducing the risk of mammary cancer and the dangers involved in taking care of large litters. It is also a known fact that males that are not neutered can become highly aggressive toward their owners and will get into fights with other males as they search for females. For these reasons and in order to avoid the killing of thousands of stray cats and dogs, the Israeli Parliament passed a law promoting the reduction of births in cats and dogs.

Although sterilizing animals is in principle forbidden by Jewish law, there are authoritative grounds to allow sterilizing cats and dogs (especially female ones), because of the Jewish law to avoid cruelty to animals. From a Jewish point of view, sterilization through medication would be completely acceptable.

One is permitted to sterilize an animal if there is medical need and castration will save the animal's life or heal it from illness. Today the number of unwanted cats and dogs in the United States is growing ever larger each day. To allow the cat and dog population to grow, only to turn unwanted animals over to shelters that routinely euthanize them because they cannot find suitable homes for them, seems terribly cruel. It is also medical opinion that spayed and neutered animals tend to live healthier and longer lives. It would thus seem that these procedures ought to be considered to be in the best interests of the animals and therefore encouraged.

6. *Do the laws of Sabbath rest include animals? Can a cow be milked on the Sabbath?*

The answer to your question is in the fourth of the Ten Commandments (Exodus 20:10), which specifically instructs us to allow our animals to rest on the Sabbath. Rabbinic authorities understand this law to include not allowing them to labor for the benefit of their owners on the Sabbath.

It is thus prohibited to place any kind of burden on an animal on the Sabbath. There are some extremely traditionally-minded Jews who will choose to not even handle animals on the Sabbath, since they are in the category of what is known as *muktzeh* (something which may not be handled because such activity serves no obvious purpose on the Sabbath). Other more moderate authorities extend a leniency to all household pets, and many will permit one to take their pet for a walk on the Sabbath.

Farmers are permitted to engage in some normally forbidden acts on the Sabbath if such actions are considered necessary to alleviate the pain and suffering of an animal. It is considered preferable, though, to engage non-Jewish workers to milk one's cows on the Sabbath because it is painful for an animal not to be milked regularly. Of course, one may certainly assist an animal on the Sabbath if it finds itself in a situation of distress (e.g., falls into a hole) and cannot free itself. And one is certainly permitted to assist an animal on the Sabbath in the process of giving birth!

7. Am I allowed to raise a pet that some people consider especially dangerous?

The Torah (Exodus 21:35) cites the case of a person's ox that injures his neighbor's ox, which eventually dies. The owner is then required to pay only partial damages for the injury caused to the neighbor's ox, because the ox had no previous history of being aggressive. But if the ox had a previous history of goring, the owner's responsibility would be one hundred percent. The reason for this is that the owner knows that the animal has violent inclinations, and if he chooses to keep the animal alive, he bears both a moral and legal responsibility for any future injuries the animal inflicts. Similarly, were a person to raise an animal that could prove dangerous to human beings, rabbinic consensus would say that it was better never to do so, because of its potential threat to other animals and human beings as well.

Maimonides rules as follows in cases of animals prone to cause damage: "Five species of animals are considered prone to cause damage from the beginning of their existence. This applies even if they have been domesticated. Thus, if they cause damage or death by goring, biting, treading, lying down upon, or the like, the owner is liable for the entire amount of the damage. They are a wolf, lion, bear, tiger, and leopard. Similarly a snake that bites, even if it has been domesticated." (Book of Damages to Property, 1:6)

For Jewish people, family and community are extremely important. One is expected to love one's neighbor as oneself, and thus we have the responsibility to be good neighbors. This would include ensuring that we would not cause any damage to our neighbor's home, grounds, and the like. It would also include choosing not to mow our lawns as the sun comes up, with the possibility of awakening our neighbors and not allowing them to complete their night of sleep. If one owns a pet, it would also mean that one would not allow one's pet to run outside unleashed, possibly leaving waste in a neighbor's yard. Several places the Talmud (Shabbat 63a and Ketubot 41b) prohibit keeping especially vicious animals in our homes. Here the concern is both for the protection of our neighbor and the protection of the household itself and those who come to visit. There is no greater gift than the gift of life itself, and therefore one must be certain when owning a pet that it is the kind of pet not likely to cause harm to another human being.

8. *If you see both a dog and a person that you do not know drowning, who should you try to save first?*

The duty of saving an endangered life (called in Hebrew *pikuach nefesh*) suspends the operation of all of the commandments in the Torah, with the exception of three prohibitions: no person is to save one's life at the price of murder, adultery, or idolatry. The Talmudic rabbis interpret the word "he shall live by them" (Leviticus 8:5) to mean that the divine commands are to be a means of life and not of death. Specifically, the duty of saving a life even supersedes the Sabbath itself, and one may do work on the Sabbath to save a life.

There is another biblical law that states that a person "shall not stand idly by the blood of your neighbor." There is a famous rabbinic dictum that says: "One who saves one's soul, it is as if that person saved the entire world." There are times when, in order to save a life, it is even considered meritorious to take the law into one's own hands and shameful to refrain from doing it. Thus there certainly would be an obligation if one sees someone in danger of drowning to hasten that person's rescue. However, a human life in this case would take precedence over the life of an animal. Obviously what would be most preferable is if it were possible to save both the human life and the animal from drowning in the scenario that you describe.

9. *According to Judaism, do animals have rights?*

It is clear to me that animals do have rights. For example, the Jewish dietary laws allow us to eat animals, but only if they are slaughtered in the most humane way possible. Additionally, Jews are only permitted to kill an animal for the express purpose of using it for food. Thus Jews are taught not to look upon the sport of hunting simply as an opportunity to get out into the open air and renew one's contact with nature. The deliberate shooting of an animal for no other reason than sport ought to be viewed negatively.

The Bible also forbids us to cause pain to any living thing. We may have pets, but only if we treat them with compassion and kindness. Interestingly enough, one Jewish tradition treats kindness to animals as a greater act of goodness than even helping one's neighbor, for we know that it cannot be done in the hope of receiving a reward in return.

In recent years there has been more and more animal experimentation. Authorities would generally permit such medical experimentation with animals if it can be sufficiently demonstrated that human life may be saved eventually as a result of doing them. Rabbinic authorities would also question the use of animal fur to create warm coats. Normally a blessing is said when one puts on new clothing, but the blessing is omitted if the clothes are made of fur.

There are still others who feel so strongly that animals have rights that they have decided to become vegetarians. In fact, God's initial intention was that people become vegetarians. The foremost Jewish Bible commentator, Rashi, wrote that "God did not permit Adam and his wife to kill a creature and to eat its flesh. Only every green herb shall they eat together." From this verse other commentators deduced that people are permitted to use animals, employ them for work, have them as pets, but not hold their life cheap nor slaughter them for food. In other words, better to be a vegetarian and leave the animals alone.

Despite the Bible's permission to eat meat, when the Jewish prophets imagined what life would be like in the messianic age, they assumed that the creatures would be herbivorous. The Prophet Isaiah envisioned a time when "the wolf shall dwell with the lamb, the leopard lie down with the kid. The cow and the bear shall graze, their young shall lie down together, and the lion, like the ox, shall eat straw." (Isaiah 11:6-7) To Isaiah, like in the Garden of Eden, the idea of having God's creatures killed for food is unthinkable.

10. *Is it okay to be involved in recreational fishing?*

While the Jewish people have not been known to embrace the hunting of animals for sport, they do frequently engage in recreational fishing. Perhaps it is due to the fact that by Jewish law any animal that is killed in hunting is automatically deemed unfit for use, because it has not been ritually slaughtered in a most humane way. Fish, however, are in a different category. First of all, they are a lower form of life than an animal, and therefore subjected to few restrictions. As long as they possess fins and scales, they are considered kosher and may be eaten. There are no Jewish laws concerning the killing of fish, though the mandate against causing unnecessary pain to a living creature would apply to fish as well. I am by no means an expert on fish and do not know the reason why fish that have fins and scales are considered kosher. I once heard from one of my students, who spoke to a marine biologist. He suggested that fish that have fins and scales tend to swim in "schools" with other fish, and that fish that swim in "schools" tend to be more passive and put up less of a fight when hooked by a fisherman. If this were the case, it would then be that less pain would be caused to such fish which are passive when hooked on a fishing line.

In recent times, new problems have arisen in the fishing industry of which you ought to be aware. Dolphins, for instance, non-kosher aquatic mammals, often swim above schools of tuna. When fishermen cast their nets for tuna, dolphins can often be accidentally caught in the nets, dying in the process. Today one can look for and easily find dolphin-safe tuna for sale.

II. *What does Jewish law say about the genetic altering of an animal? Can a non-kosher animal ever be made to be kosher?*

I came across an interesting book called *Baxter, the Pig Who Wanted to be Kosher.* And very recently a congregant asked whether it would ever be permissible for a Jew who keeps kosher to eat a pig if it could be genetically altered. (Pigs have cloven hooves, but do not chew their cud, and need both these attributes in order to be considered kosher.) In recent years, modern science has successfully been able to genetically alter both animal and plant life by manipulating the DNA found in the cells of living organisms. This is generally done to make the organisms heartier. For example, Israel has been able to create a heartier tomato that will be able to be exported with less damage to the tomato. Theoretically, it may eventually be possible to create new forms of animal life through genetic manipulation.

The Committee of Law and Standards of the Rabbinical Assembly (the union of Rabbis of which I am a member) has a responsum by Rabbi Avram I. Reisner. Rabbi Reisner rules that adding genetic material from a non-kosher animal to a kosher animal does not change the status of the kosher animal to make it non-kosher. This is because the material being transferred is sub-microscopic and the laws of forbidden mixtures tolerate minute amounts of forbidden substances. Obviously, one must always consider the potential risks to human health of anything that is genetically altered.

About twenty years ago I remember reading that a kosher pig was found in the wilds of Indonesia. This pig-like creature had split hooves and chewed its cud. Because pig has always been considered such an abhorrent creature in the Jewish traditional world, I would highly doubt whether Jews who keep kosher would ever consider indulging in a genetically altered pig that had split hooves and now chewed its cud. For this answer, we will just have to wait and see.

12. *Is it right to ask a rabbi to say the special gomel prayer for a safe recovery for a pet that was nearly run over in an auto accident but survived?*

Persons who have safely returned from some hazardous voyage or recovered from a serious illness or accident are encouraged to offer thanks to God in the form of a benediction recited in addition to the Torah blessings when called to the public reading of the Torah in the synagogue. The benediction is known as *Birkat ha-gomel*, and is derived from Psalm 107, according to a Talmudic interpretation. (Talmud, Berachot 54b). Psalm 107 begins by calling upon the exiles, brought back to their homes, to give thanks. Then it describes God's goodness in taking care of lost travelers, prisoners, the sick, and sea voyagers. The refrain at the end of each of the four stanzas reads: "Let them thank God for his kindness and His wonders toward humanity." The blessing in translation is: "Praised are You, God, Ruler of the Universe, who bestows favor on the undeserving and has shown me every kindness." Upon hearing the blessing, the entire congregation responds: "May the One who has shown you every kindness ever deal kindly with you."

Saying thank you is an important value in Jewish tradition, and I have had several experiences in my life that warranted my saying the *Birkat ha-gomel*. There is no question in my mind that if your pet has made a full recovery from a serious illness, operation, and the like that saying this benediction on behalf of your pet would be a good idea. All one would have to do is slightly alter the traditional blessing. So I suggest the following:

"Praised are You, Adonai Our God, Ruler of the Universe, who has shown goodness to my beloved pet (include name) and therefore grace upon me."

Congregation Responds: "May God who has been gracious to you and your pet continue to favor both of you with all that is good."

13. *Is it true that there is no special blessing for buying a pair of new shoes or a garment made of fur? Why is this so?*

Judaism has a unique blessing called the *shehecheyanu* that reads: "Praised are You, Adonai our God, Ruler of the Universe, who has granted us life and sustenance and permitted us to reach this festive occasion." It is traditionally recited when tasting new fruit for the first time in the season, when moving into a new house, when lighting the first *Hanukkah* candle, when becoming a Bar or Bat Mitzvah, and when putting on a new garment for the first time. The idea behind the blessing is to show appreciation to God for a moment of transition in your life.

When a person wears a new garment for the first time, it is also Jewish custom to say to him or her, "Wear it out and renew it – *t'valleh u-t'chaddeish*." However, there are rabbinic authorities who firmly state that one should not say this (or the *shehecheyanu*) in the case of new shoes or other garments that are made from animal hides and fur. The reason is that this implies a necessity eventually to kill another animal from which to acquire the pelt with which to renew the garment in question, whereas it is written in the Bible that God's mercy is over all of God's works. Interestingly, there is also a custom of not reciting the *shehecheyanu* when acquiring a new Torah scroll, since parchment is written on animal skin. And during the period of mourning when a Jew sits *shiva*, the custom is that the mourner should not wear leather shoes but rather shoes made of cloth, in order to show compassion to animals and to remind the mourner that the life of an animal is sacrificed for the shoes that one wears.

14. *My best friend (not married) passed away. He owned a dog, and I was wondering whether I am under any Jewish obligation to adopt his dog?*

The loss of any human being is painful, especially one's best friend. The Talmud (Shevuot 39a) says that all Jews are responsible one for another. And the great Rabbi Hillel wrote, "If I am only for myself, what am I?" (Ethics of the Fathers, 1:14) Certainly you would have an obligation to reach out to the family (your friend's siblings, if he had any, parents, and the like) to see in which way you could be of assistance. However, you yourself would not be obliged to inherit his pet. Your friend's family members would of course want to be sure to seek out a suitable home for the dog, and possibly take the dog to become their own family member. If unable to do so for whatever reason, you might want to assist in searching for a suitable home for the pet by seeking out your other friends and acquaintances and getting their feedback and advice. And, of course, as a best friend, you will likely choose to eulogize your friend and do all that you can to help comfort the bereaved family and work to perpetuate your friend's memory.

15. *Does Jewish law permit animal experimentation?*

Animal rights advocates often claim, contrary to popular opinion, that experimentation on animals is hardly ever necessary and is of limited value to understanding human biological processes. Others reject this argument as being misleading. Rabbinic opinion varies with regard to your question of animal experimentation. One view suggests that although there is no basis in Jewish law for a legal ban on such experiments, they are morally indefensible. A refuting view asserts that the pain of the animal surely counts less than the pain of sick people who might be helped by such research. This appears to be the prevailing view, provided that all reasonable steps are taken to prevent any unnecessary suffering and to limit the practice strictly to the advancement of human health. It also must be clear that some clear benefit come to humans from the testing.

1. *Can you tell me if and where dogs appear in the Torah?*

The derivation of the Hebrew word *kelev* (dog) is unknown. Some have suggested that Hebrew is connected with *kalav*, meaning to make stitches resembling dog bites. There are only two places in the Torah where dogs are mentioned. In one (Exodus 22:3) we are told, "You shall not eat the meat of an animal that was torn in the field, to the dog shall you throw it." Eating the meat of a kosher animal that has been savaged by a wild animal is considered a loathsome act, for the Torah only permits the consumption of meat from an animal that has been slaughtered in the most humane ritual manner.

In biblical days the dog had a bad reputation. Dogs were undomesticated, wild, and ferocious. They were also street scavengers. The other dog reference in the Torah is Exodus 11:7, where it says concerning the Israelites' departure from Egypt that God promises that the Exodus will be so unopposed that "not even a dog will bark." The eleventh century commentator Rashi notes how these verses are one way in which God assures us that the guilty ultimately receive their punishment, just as the righteous receive their reward. Because the dogs were silent and did not bark during the Exodus from Egypt – allowing the Israelites to leave without the annoyance of any disturbance, God rewarded the dogs by declaring that meat from injured animals should be thrown to them. In other words, if God rewards such actions from animals, God will certainly reward human actions.

There are other references to dogs in the other books of the Hebrew Bible. The shepherd dog is referred to in the Book of Job 30:1: "Whose fathers I disdained to set with the dogs of my flock." The Book of Isaiah speaks of "dumb dogs that cannot bark." (Isaiah 56:10)

When we turn to the Talmud and Midrash we find the same pattern of both complimentary and uncomplimentary remarks regarding the dog. Because the preservation of life was always emphasized, we are warned not to handle a wild dog (Midrash, Genesis Rabbah 77), nor to tolerate a mad dog, which was permitted to be killed even on the Sabbath (Talmud, Shabbat 121b). We are also advised not to raise a bad dog in the house, as this would be a transgression of Deuteronomy 22:8: "You shall not bring blood upon your house." (Talmud Baba Kamma 15b)

The Rabbis even diagnosed the symptoms of rabies: "Its mouth open, its saliva dripping, its ears flap, its tail hanging between its thighs, and it walks on the edge of the road. Some say it barks without its voice being heard." (Talmud Yoma 83b)

Finally, Ecclesiastes declared: "A living dog is better than a dead lion." (Ecclesiastes 9:4). The exposition of this verse is discussed in the Talmud. When King David died on the holy Sabbath, his son Solomon sent a message to the House of Study: "My father is dead and lying in the sun, and the dogs of my father's house are hungry, what shall I do?" The reply quickly came: "Cut up a carcass and place it before the dogs, and as for your father, carry him away." (Talmud Shabbat 30b)

2. *What makes for a clean or unclean animal in the Torah?*

The kosher laws enumerating which animals, fowl, and fish are permitted, and which are forbidden, have their basis in the Five Books of Moses. Leviticus 11:44-45 are two important chapters in this regard. Edible animals (called clean or pure in the Torah) are those that have cloven hooves and chew their cud. These would include such animals as sheep, cows, buffalo, goats, and deer. Aquatic animals that lack fins and scales, such as eels, shrimp, and crabs, are non-edible. Birds of prey and carrion eaters are unclean and forbidden as food. Permitted fowl include chicken, duck, goose, pigeon, and turkey. Animals must be properly slaughtered by a competent Jewish ritual slaughterer in order to be eaten. If an animal dies by itself or is killed by a human or another animal, it is non-edible. Every time a Jew sits down to eat a kosher meal, he or she is reminded that the animal to be eaten is a creature of God, that the death of such a creature cannot be taken lightly, and that we cannot treat any living thing irresponsibly.

3. *What are some of the animals that appear in the Bible?*

There are more than 120 names of animals in the Bible, representing mammals, birds, and reptiles in particular. Following is an alphabetical summary of some of the biblical animals and their sources:

Addax (Deuteronomy 14:4)

Ant (Proverbs 6:6-8)

Ass (Genesis 12:16)

Bat (Leviticus 11:19)

Bear (1 Samuel 17:34-37)

Bee (Deuteronomy 1:24)

Beetle (Jonah 4:7)

Bison (Deuteronomy 14:15)

Boar (Psalm 80:14)

Buffalo (Second Samuel 6:13)

Camel (Genesis 12:16)

Cattle (Genesis 13:5)

Cobra (Deuteronomy 32:33)

Cock (Job 38:36)

Crane (Isaiah 38:14)

Deer (Deuteronomy 14:5)

Dog (Exodus 22:30)

Dove Genesis 8:8)

Eagle (Genesis 15:11)

Fox (Lamentations 5:18)

Frog (Exodus 7:27)

Gazelle (Deuteronomy 12:15)

Gecko (Leviticus 11:30)

Goat (Leviticus 7:23)

Goose (First Kings 5:3)

Grasshopper (Leviticus 11:22)

Hawk (Leviticus 11:16)

Hippo (Job 40:15)

Horse (Exodus 9:3)

Hyena (First Samuel 13:18)

Ibex (Psalm 104:18)

Jackal (Judges 15:4)

Leopard (Isaiah 11:6)

Lion (Isaiah 38:13)

Lizard (Leviticus 11:30)

Locust (Exodus 10:11)

Louse (Isaiah 51:6)

Monkey (First Kings 10:22)

Mouse (Leviticus 11:29)

Nightingale (Song of Songs 2:12)

Ostrich (Lamentations 4:3)

Owl (Isaiah 13:21)

Ox (Numbers 23:22)

Partridge (Numbers 26:33)

Peacock (First Kings 10:22)

Quail (Exodus 16:13)

Rat (Leviticus 11:29)

Raven (Genesis 8:7)

Scorpion (Deuteronomy 8:15)

Sheep (Genesis 4:2)

Snake (Genesis 3:1)

Sparrow (Leviticus 14:4)

Spider (Isaiah 59:5)

Swine (Leviticus 11:7)

Vulture (Leviticus 11:13)

Wasp (Exodus 23:28)

Whale (Psalm 104:26)

Wolf (Isaiah 11:6)

4. Why did God create animals in the first place?

Before God is described as creating man and woman in the second chapter of the Book of Genesis, God says that "it is not good for man to be alone. I will make a fitting helper for him." (Genesis 2:18) Following this statement God forms all of the animals and birds, and brings them to man to see what he would call them. And whatever man called each living creature, that would be its name. This was the first independent decision that man was able to make by himself. In the ancient world, to know something's inner name was to know its nature and have power over it. By having Adam give names to the animals, God is again showing us in the story of creation that the human being is more than an animal. Unlike animals, humans have the power of speech. By giving the animals their names, man shows his dominion over them. And just as God has dominion over humans and often treats us with compassion, we have to treat animals with love and compassion.

Perhaps God created the animals because God thought it was not good for the man to be alone and wanted him to have a complement. However, with animals as part of the creation, Adam comes to realize that none of the animals were good to be his mate, and all of the animals had mates except for him. Adam had to experience for himself his own loneliness in order to understand his need for a mate.

In addition, animals were created to help man in his work, and in the time of Noah we also learn that they are permitted to be eaten as well. Since man has learned to enjoy the taste of meat and fish, we have yet another reason for God's creation of the animal kingdom.

5. *What does it means when the Torah says that "man was created in God's image" but the animals were not?*

In Genesis 9:26 it says: "And God said, Let us make man in our image, after our likeness. They shall rule the fish of the sea, the birds of the sky, the cattle, the whole earth and all the creeping things that creep on the earth." Since the Jewish God is without image and form, rabbinic commentators in every generation have been puzzled over the plural language in this verse. Jewish legend (Genesis Rabbah 8:5) explains that God consulted with the angels, perhaps hinting at a measure of divine ambivalence. Truth and Peace oppose creating humans on the grounds that they would ultimately be deceitful and contentious. Love and Righteousness favor their creation, for without humanity, how can there be love and righteousness in the world? God sides with those favoring creation. Some commentary has posited that God was speaking to the animals: Together let us fashion a unique image (yours and Mine), a creature like an animal in some ways – needing to eat, sleep, and mate, and like God in some ways – capable of compassion, morality, and self-consciousness.

According to Professor Aviva Zornberg, animals and insects expand horizontally – to "fill" the earth. Humans grow vertically – to "master" the earth and serve as its custodians, by changing, controlling, and improving their environment.

The word "image" is a metaphor, and does not refer to God as physical in form. Rather, I concur with many modern commentators that the creation of man formed in God's image reflects the Bible's abiding wonder over a human's special stature in creation, including his unique intellectual and moral capacity which bears the imprint of the Creator. The likeness also describes a person's moral potential and ability to use reason to guide his actions, which is limited in the animal kingdom. Man's nature is radically different from God's, but man is capable of approaching God's actions: God's love, mercy, and justice. Man becomes a true human being when he attempts to do godly deeds.

Dr. Jeffrey Tigay, in his commentary on the Book of Genesis (JPS Torah Commentary, p. 12), posits that to describe man as made in God's image is to elevate the status and infinite worth of a human being, affirming the inviolability of the human person. It also asserts human dominance over the animal kingdom.

6. *What animals are used as symbols of the Tribes of Israel?*

There are traditionally twelve Hebrew tribes, representing each of the sons of Jacob. According to Genesis, his sons were: Reuben, Simeon, Levi, Judah, Issachar, Zebulun, Benjamin, Dan, Naphtali, Gad, Asher, and Joseph. Some, however, say that Reuben lost his rights as firstborn by defiling Jacob's bed, and in place of Reuben and Joseph we have Joseph's two sons, Ephraim and Manasseh. Here are the signs mentioning animals often depicted in synagogue art, based on their description in the Book of Genesis, chapter 49:

> Judah is a lion's whelp (49:9)
> Issachar is a strong-boned ass (49:14)
> Dan is a serpent by the road and viper by the path (49:17)
> Naphtali is a hind let loose (49:21)
> Joseph is a wild ass (49:22)
> Benjamin is a ravenous wolf (49:27)

Each of the animals describes a characteristic of the person. The lion's whelp of Judah is a metaphor for strength and daring. The strong-boned ass description of Issachar is meant to imply a criticism of the tribe for placing its strength in the service of Canaanites. Dan as a serpent and viper by the path may allude to the form of guerilla warfare to which it resorted in battle. The hind of Naphtali is a symbol of beauty, while the wild ass image of Joseph is often understood to allude to the freedom and independence of the Joseph tribes. Finally, the wolf imagery of Benjamin is meant to portray him as a warrior.

7. Are there instances in the Bible when God blesses an animal?

On the fifth day of creation we are told that God created the living creatures of every kind, the birds, animals, insects, and sea creatures. God saw that it was good, and then in Genesis 1:22 we have the following: "God blessed them, saying, be fertile and increase, fill the waters in the seas, and let the birds increase the earth." The animal kingdom, unlike plant life (which has its own capacity for self-reproduction by nonsexual means) receives the gift of fertility through the divine blessing of sexual reproduction. In blessing the animals, God gives them their own power to produce new life even as God creates new life. The birth of any living creature is an instance of God's continuing creative power.

8. How are animals given their names in the Torah?

One of Adam's tasks after he himself is created is to give names to the animals. In addition to learning that he will be the master over the animals, God tells Adam (Genesis 2:18) that it will be his task to give each living creature its name. This is the very first independent task that Adam will get to perform in his life. Jewish legend suggests that God first went to the angels to give names to the animals. When they were not successful He next went to Adam, who succeeded in naming all of the animals, thus demonstrating his superior intelligence, or at least advanced knowledge of zoology, at this point obviously a very young science.

But there is a deeper interpretation here. In the ancient world, to know something's inner name was to know its true nature – to have power over it. By having Adam give names to the animals, God is again showing us in this story that the human being is more than an animal. Unlike animals, humans have the power of speech. By giving the animals their names, he shows his dominion over them.

9. *What are the biblical commands related to showing kindness to animals?*

Kindly treatment of animals is legislated in the Ten Commandments. The fourth commandment rules: "The seventh day is a Sabbath of God; you shall not do any work – you, your son, your daughter, your ox or ass, or any of your cattle . . ." (Deuteronomy 5:14) Thus animals, too, like humans, were afforded the privilege of Sabbath rest.

Under the heading of the prevention of cruelty to animals, other laws in the Torah regulated that an animal could not be muzzled while working in the field (Deuteronomy 25:4), so that it could eat all that it wanted. Also: "You shall not plow an ox and mule harnessed together" (Deuteronomy 22:10), since being of unequal size and strength both animals would suffer pain and hardship. Another example: When a man comes across a bird nest, he cannot slaughter the mother bird with the young, but must send her away (Deuteronomy 22:6), for the pain of the mother under such circumstances is very substantial. Centuries later the Talmudic rabbis legislated that one is forbidden to eat one's meal before he has given food to his own animals. (Talmud Berachot 40a)

In addition, the Jewish laws of kosher slaughtering regulate that an animal must be killed in the most humane way possible. Using a sharp blade and a single stroke, this method minimizes the suffering of an animal.

In today's world, the laws of preventing cruelty to animals would also prohibit wearing the skins of baby seals that have been clubbed to death or eating an animal that has been known to be kept in cages in order to produce its special tasting meat (i.e., veal from a baby calf).

Moses Cordovero, in *The Palm Tree of Deborah*, sums up this law of preventing animal cruelty in this way: Compassion should be extended to all creatures, neither destroying nor despising any of them. For God's wisdom is extended to all created things: minerals, plants, animals, and humans. This is the reason the rabbis warned us against despising food. In this way, a person's pity should be extended to all of the works of the Holy Blessed One, just as in God's wisdom, nothing is to be despised. One should not uproot anything which grows unless it is necessary, nor kill any living thing unless it is necessary. And one should choose a good death for them with a knife that has been carefully examined, to have pity on them as far as it is possible.

10. *What was the purpose of sacrificing animals as described in the Torah?*

Animal sacrifices were to the Jews of biblical times what worship and prayer are to their modern descendants. They both provided a way for our people to communicate and speak to God. About 150 of the 613 Torah laws deal with sacrifices.

Throughout the ancient world, people connected with their gods in part through sacrifice. Altars abounded and received all kinds of animals. It is therefore not surprising that the Bible, too, is filled with instances of altars used as vehicles for sacrifice. In biblical times, sacrifices were generally intended to obtain God's favor and atone for the sins of the sacrifice. They also demonstrated one's submission to God and served as recognition of God's power. Although libation of wine and meal offerings played a prominent role in some of the biblical rituals, the most important biblical sacrifices were those of animals. The sacrificial animal had to be free of all blemishes, domesticated, and had to be the property of the person who was offering the sacrifice.

Following is a brief summary of biblical sacrifices and the animals that were used to accompany them.

Propitiatory Offerings: Two offerings belong to this category: the sin offering, called a *chattat*, and the guilt offering, called an *asham*. The sin offering was suited to the rank and the circumstance of the person who offered it. Thus, the High Priest brought a young bull (Leviticus 4:3), a *nasi* (ruler) brought a male goat (Leviticus 4:23), and a commoner would bring a female goat (Leviticus 4:28) or a lamb (Leviticus 4:32). A sin offering of one male goat was required at each of the sacred festivals, including the New Moon (Numbers 28:15), Passover (Numbers 25:22-24), Shavuot (Numbers 28:30), Rosh Hashanah (Numbers 29:5), the Day of Atonement (Numbers 29:11), and each day of the Festival of Sukkot (Numbers 29:16,19).

Rites of purification called for a lesser sin offering. For instance, lambs or birds were used after childbirth (Leviticus 12:6-8), leprosy (Leviticus 14:12-14), and unclean issues. (Leviticus 15:5).

The guilt offering was a special kind of sin offering (Leviticus 5:7) that was required when persons had been denied their rightful due. In addition to the reparation of the amount defrauded, plus a fine of 20 percent (Leviticus 5:16-24), guilty persons had to bring a guilt offering, usually a ram.

Burnt Offerings: In Hebrew, *olah*, meaning "to go up", this sacrifice made use of these animals: bulls, sheep or goats, and birds (Leviticus 1:3-7). A continual burnt offering (known as an *olah tamid*), consisting of a male lamb that was sacrificed both morning and evening (Exodus 29:38-42), was made twice daily during biblical times. Two additional lambs were offered each Sabbath (Numbers 28:9-10). There were no sin offerings that accompanied the burnt offering sacrifices. On the other hand, a sin offering of one goat was required along with the burnt offerings on the other holy days. Bulls, lambs, and rams were the primary animals used for the burnt offerings.

Peace Offerings: Called *shelamim* in Hebrew, this type of offering was the most basic of all communal sacrifices. Any domesticated animal was allowed to be used as a peace offering, which always concluded with some type of communal meal. The peace offering was specified only for the celebration of Shavuot (Leviticus 23:19-20), in the ritual for the completion of a Nazarite vow (Numbers 6:17-20), and at the installation of the priests (Exodus 29:19-34). National events that called for the peace offering included the successful completion of a military campaign (First Samuel 11:15), the end of a famine (Second Samuel 24:25), and the praising of a candidate for the kingship. (First Kings 1:9).

The various branches of Judaism have distinctive ways of relating to the sacrifices of bygone years which took place in Temple times. Reform Judaism has simply dropped the subject of sacrifices. The Orthodox prayerbook reiterates the hope that one day the Jerusalem Temple will be rebuilt and sacrifices offered there one again. The Conservative prayerbook has changed all future references of sacrifices to the past tense, expressing no desire to have them reconstituted.

11. *What are some of the talking animals in the Bible?*

The first of the talking creatures presented in the Five Books of Moses is the talking serpent. It is the serpent that is able to convince Adam to eat the forbidden fruit in the Book of Genesis. The association of serpents with guile is an old one. In ancient Mesopotamian myths, serpents oppose the will of the gods. When God prohibits Adam and Eve from eating of the tree of knowledge of good and evil, the shrewd and strangely talkative serpent tells Eve that if she eats of the tree she will be just as knowledgeable as God: "God knows that as soon as you eat it, your eyes will be opened and you will be like God." (Genesis 3:5) Eve does eat from the tree, as does Adam, and as their punishment, they are banned forever from the Garden of Eden and must earn their own living.

There are many rabbinic interpretations of this story. Some see it as representing the eternal encounter between animal nature (driven by instinct and physical attractiveness) and human nature capable of saying no to temptation. Some commentators see the serpent as jealous of the special status of the humans, and determined to cause a breach between them and God. Some see it as the embodiment of sexual temptation, the serpent being a phallic image and the tree of knowledge referring to the sexual awareness that accompanies coming of age.

If the serpent truly represents something within the human soul rather than outside of it, that would certainly explain why it alone of all the animals has the power of speech.

The second talking animal is the talking donkey in the Book of Numbers. Mr. Ed, the talking horse of TV fame in the 1960's, apparently was not an original. Long before the advent of television the Bible had its own talking animal: Balaam's donkey. The story of Balak, Balaam, and his talking donkey is one of the most fascinating and intriguing in all of the Torah. Balak, King of Moab, fears that the Israelites will attack his country. Balak thus decides to send for Balaam, a pagan prophet known for his special powers to bless and curse. Balak promises to richly reward Balaam for cursing Israel, and Balaam takes some time to consider the offer. During the night God tells Balaam that he must not curse the Israelites, for they are a people who are blessed. Later on in the story, God tells Balaam to go with the messengers, but to say only what God commands.

Balaam sets out for Moab on his donkey. At this point, a macabre dialogue in the Bible ensues. God opens the mouth of the donkey, and she finally says to Balaam, "What have I done to you that you have beaten me these three times?" Finally, God opens Balaam's eyes, and he sees the angel of God standing in front of him with a drawn sword. The angel scolds Balaam for striking his donkey, and Balaam, realizing how God opposes his mission to curse the Israelites, tries to pacify him. Finally, the angel permits Balaam to resume his journey on the one condition that he will say only what God tells him. Instead of damning the Israelites, Balaam blesses them, promising that the Israelites will triumph over all of their enemies, including the Moabites.

What I have personally found astonishing in this strange story (Numbers 22-24) is the absence of concern about Balaam's treatment of the donkey. Balaam's behavior and the donkey's response translate in our modern day to an issue of empowerment. What we learn from the donkey is clear: if we are on the receiving end of any kind of abuse, we have an obligation to speak out firmly against our abuser. The story of Balaam and his talking donkey provide an important model of an abuser, reacting by venting misdirected anger in verbal abuse or physical violence, and the recipient of his abuse, finally deciding that she has had enough.

In the rabbinic book Ethics of Our Fathers we are told that Balaam's donkey was one of ten miraculous things that God created at twilight just before the first Sabbath. It appears then that the donkey was created for this one time use in the Book of Numbers, and that there will never again be another talking donkey.

12. *What is the meaning of all of the animals mentioned in the Chad Gadya song sung at the end of the Passover Seder?*

One of the fun songs at the Passover seder is Chad Gadya, meaning "one goat." It is intended for the entertainment of all the participants and is an enjoyable song to sing. The Chad Gadya poem has ten stanzas which are written in a nursery style rhyme and phrased in Aramaic. The song is generally interpreted as an allegory which describes the trials and difficulties of the Israelite journey throughout Jewish history. Each object symbolizes one of Israel's enemies, and some of the objects are animals. Here is one interpretation of all of the players in the Chad Gadya song:

Israel	(the only goat)
Adonai	(the father)
Zuzim	(Ten Commandment tablets)
Cat	(Assyria)

<pre>
         Dog   (Babylon)
         Stick   (Persia)
         Fire   (Greece)
        Water   (Rome)
           Ox   (Saracens)
   Slaughterer   (Crusaders)
Angel of Death   (Ottomans)
</pre>

In the end the Holy Blessed One saves the entire Jewish people.

A great idea to enhance the singing of this song is for participants to take each character in the song and create a sound for the character as the character is being sung. For example, each time that the cat is mentioned, someone says "meow," when the dog is mentioned "bow wow," and so on.

13. *I have always been disturbed by the story in Deuteronomy of breaking the neck of a heifer and sacrificing it for atonement. It seems insensitive and cruel to me and I was wondering about its purpose and message?*

The story of the red heifer (*parah adumah*) first occurs in the Book of Numbers (chapter 19). It refers to the special animal, a red cow which has no defect or blemish and has never been worked, whose ashes were used in the ritual purification of persons and objects defiled by a corpse. Unlike ordinary animal sacrifices, the red heifer was only allowed to be slaughtered outside of the camp, and its ashes were to be burned with a mixture of cedar wood, hyssop, and scarlet, cast upon the pyre. The gathered ashes, dissolved in fresh water, were to be sprinkled on those who had become contaminated through contact with the dead.

The law of the red heifer is a classic example of a law that defies rational explanation and is one of the most mysterious. The original intent of the law in the Bible was to purify the defiled, and yet it defiled all of those who were in any way connected with the preparation of the ashes and the water purification.

The need to be cleansed after touching a corpse reflected an ancient and universal fear of the dead, whose spirits were believed to be capable of injuring people. Some commentators assert that the ritual of the red heifer is undoubtedly based on pre-biblical practices. (An old Canaanite epic tells of the death of the god of fertility, who went to the underworld and there copulated with a heifer.)

The idea clearly presented in the story of the red heifer is that Israelites are a holy people and that holiness demands a state of both physical and spiritual purity. Israelites must eat "clean" foods, and if they touch anything upon which a taboo rests, such as dead people or animals unfit for food, they become tainted and must wait until a certain time has elapsed to have their pristine condition restored.

Most difficult of all the aspects of the ritual is the provision that handling the ashes renders the person impure. A Jewish legend (Tanchuma, Chukkat 26) relates that a gentile once came to Rabbi Yochanan ben Zakki and asked about the reason for the ritual. The rabbi gave him a rational answer but later admitted to his students that a mystery was involved, for in and of themselves the dead were not impure, nor the ashes purifying. "But," said the sage, "this is what God has decreed, and you may not transgress the law."

In another explanation of the symbolism of the ingredients mixed with the red heifer ashes, the majestic cedar of Lebanon was said to be the symbol of pride and the hyssop a symbol of humility.

Be reminded that the red heifer story is always read in the synagogue several weeks before Passover. Its reading is meant to remind our people today that Passover is around the corner, and we must get ready for it by cleaning our homes, removing the leaven, and purifying ourselves.

Lastly, a very puzzling story about a heifer occurs in Deuteronomy 21:1–9. In this story, when a corpse was discovered, the nearest community was considered responsible, a heifer was chosen to be killed, and the community elders would announce "our hands did not shed this blood." Many biblical commentators have reasoned that this rite would attract so much public attention and interest that the level of communal responsibility would be raised by this procedure, and its shock value would prevent the people from forgetting the act and could keep alive the search for the offender. The Talmud reports that the procedure of breaking the neck of the heifer ceased when crimes of murder multiplied to such a degree that the ritual was no longer feasible.

14. *Can you tell me more about the goat ritual that we read about on Yom Kippur?*

Leviticus 16:8-10 presents a fascinating ritual related to Yom Kippur, the Day of Atonement. As part of the ritual, we are told that Aaron cast lots upon two goats. One lot was for God, and the other lot was for Azazel (some sort of demon). Aaron presented the goat upon which the lot fell for God, and offered it for a sin offering. But the goat on which the lot fell for Azazel, was set alive before God, and was subsequently sent away into the wilderness.

The goat that was dispatched to Azazel was not a sacrifice, since it was not slaughtered. From the biblical verse it is not even clear whether the goat was killed. The goat was dispatched as vicarious atonement to carry the sins of Israel into the wilderness. Thus the people were symbolically cleansed of their sins on the Day of Atonement.

A detailed description of the ritual during Second Temple times is found in the Mishneh in the general description of the worship service of the Day of Atonement: the High Priest cast lots – upon one the word L'YHVH ('to the Lord') and upon the other L'Azazel ("to Azazel"). After he drew lots, on the head of the goat chosen for Azazel he bound a thread of crimson wool and stood the animal opposite the gate through which it would ultimately be taken. (Talmud Yomah 4:1-2) After the High Priest had performed several other rituals, he returned to the goat, placed his hands on it, and confessed the sins of the people. The goat was then banished to the wilderness. The entire ceremony has been preserved in the traditional High Holy Day prayerbook and is a part of its liturgy.

The exact meaning of Azazel was already a point of dispute in Talmudic times. Some posited that it was the name of the place to which the goat was sent, while others believed that it was the name of some "power." The school of Rabbi Ishmael explained that it is called Azazel because it atones for the acts of the fallen angels Uzza and Azael.

There have been several attempts to compare the ritual of the goat to several customs of the ancient world. For instance, in Babylon it was customary on the festival of Akitu (New Year) to give goats as a substitute for a human being to Ereshkigal, the goddess of the abyss. During plagues, the ancient Hittites used to send a goat into the enemy territory in order that it should carry the plague there.

The word scapegoat, which today is used to denote a person who is made to bear the blame for others, is derived from the ceremony of the goats back in biblical times.

15. *I heard that there is an animal mitzvah in the Torah that promises a reward for its performance. What is it?*

There are only two Torah laws in the Five Books of Moses that promise rewards. One is in the Book of Exodus, where we are told in the Ten Commandments: "Honor your father and mother, that you may long endure on the land that God is assigning to you." (Exodus 20:12) The sages interpret this verse not to command feelings of affection but to command behavior. We are obliged to support and maintain our parents and to avoid shaming them.

The second Torah law is the one related to a bird: "When you chance upon a bird's nest, in any tree or on the ground, with fledglings or eggs and the mother sitting over the fledglings or on the eggs, do not take the mother together with her young. Let the mother go, and take only the young, in order that you may fare well and have a long life." (Deuteronomy 22:6-7) The compassion demanded for the mother bird here is one of the biblical passages that led the Sages to formulate the general principle that we must avoid causing unnecessary pain to animals.

16. *There are many covenants in the Torah between God and people. Are there any treaties or covenants between God and animals?*

After the flood in the time of Noah in the Book of Genesis, God blesses Noah and his children. Then in chapter 9 of the Book of Genesis, verses 8–10, God says: "As for Me, behold, I establish My covenant with you, and with your seed after you. And with every living creature that is with you, of all that go out of the ark, even every beast of the earth. And I will establish My covenant with you. Neither shall all flesh be cut off any more by the waters of the flood to destroy the earth. And God said: This is the token of the covenant which I make between Me and you and every living creature that is with you, for perpetual generations. I have set my bow in the cloud, and it shall be for a token of a covenant between Me and the earth."

Here we see that God not only makes a covenant with Noah and his family, but with all of the living creatures, and the sign of the covenant is the rainbow in the sky. This does not imply that the rainbow was then for the first time instituted. It merely assumed a new role as a token of God's pledge that there would never again be a world-devastating flood.

In ancient myth, a rainbow represented instruments used by the gods in battle. The bows would be hung in the sky as symbols of victory. The Hebrew word *keshet* means both rainbow and a bow of war. Seeing a rainbow, for which there is a special blessing in Judaism, is always meant to be a reminder of this eternal covenant. The blessing is: Praised are You, God, who remembers the Covenant, is faithful to it, and keeps promises. (Talmud Berachot 59a)

According to some commentary, the rainbow is a sign of peace in three ways: it represents the inverted bow, the weapon turned away so that it does not threaten. It represents all shades and colors joined side by side, calling on different races and nations to do the same. And it represents the promise that no matter how hard it may rain, the rain eventually will stop and the sun will come out again.

17. *Can you cite some examples of kindness to animals by biblical heroes?*

Many great people in the Bible were trained for their tasks by being shepherds of flocks. In the following story (Exodus Rabbah 2:2), we learn how Moses was tested by God through his shepherding:

While our teacher Moses was tending the sheep of Jethro in the desert a lamb ran away from him. He ran after her until she reached Hasuah. Upon reaching Hasuah she came upon a pool of water, whereupon the lamb stopped to drink. When Moses reached her he said, "I did not know that you were running because you were thirsty. You must be tired." He placed her on his shoulder and began to walk. The Holy Blessed One said, "You are compassionate in leading flocks belonging to mortals; I swear you will similarly shepherd my flock, Israel."

In another Jewish legend (Exodus Rabbah 2:2) we learn how God deemed David worthy of tending the Jewish people. David knew how to look after sheep, bestowing upon each the care it needed. David used to prevent the larger sheep from going out before the smaller ones. The smaller ones were then able to graze upon the tender grass. Next, he permitted the old sheep to feed from the ordinary grass, and finally the young, lusty sheep at the tougher grass.

In the Book of Genesis, (24:11-20), we learn of the kindness to animal test to which Rebekah was subjected in order to be considered suitable as a wife for Isaac, son of Abraham. In the story Eliezer, Abraham's servant, asked Rebekah for water for himself. She not only gave him water, but also ran to provide water for his camels. Rebekah's concern for camels was evidence of a tender heart and compassion for all of God's creatures. It convinced Eliezer that she would make a fine wife for Isaac.

Finally, the patriarch Jacob also demonstrated concern for animals. After their reconciliation, his brother Esau said to him, "Let us take our journey and let us go, and I will go before you." But "My lord knows that the children are tender, and that the flocks and the herds giving suck are a care to me. And if my workers overdrive them one day, all the flocks will die. Let my lord, I pray you, pass over his servant and I will journey on gently, according to the pace of the cattle that are before me and according to the pace of the children, until I come unto my lord, unto Seir." (Genesis 33:12-14)

18. *Are there any Psalms that illustrate God's close identification with the animal kingdom?*

Of the 150 Psalms, Psalm 104 may be said to paint a picture of the entire cosmos. Beasts and wild asses are described in verse 11 of being quenched by rainwater of the springs. Birds are described as nesting in the cedars of Lebanon (v. 16), while storks use fir trees for their houses (v. 17). The high mountains are described as places for the wild goats (v. 18), and the young lions (v. 21) seek their food from God, roaring for their prey. The Psalm has a wonderful ending:

I will sing unto God as long as I live. (v. 33) In other words, because throughout the remainder of the life of the Psalmist his mind will be so impressed by his consciousness of God's marvelous works, he will sing.

Psalm 23, known as the Lord is my Shepherd, is the psalm par excellence of comfort. In this Psalm God is portrayed as the faithful shepherd and protector of His sheep (i.e., His people). The Psalm is staged on green pastures where in the heat of the sun the people are led to cool meadows.

Finally, Psalm 29 describes the majesty of God in the storm, where God makes Mount Lebanon skip like a calf, compelling Siryon to leap like a ram. In other words, the whole earth trembles in the presence of God's powerful voice.

Lifecycle

1. *Do animals have souls?*

The Hebrew word *nefesh* (soul) is used in many senses. It has different shades of meaning at different times. It denotes the principle of life, the thing that constitutes a living being. Man became a human being in the Book of Genesis (2:7) when God "breathed into his nostrils the breath of life and gave man his soul." Since God is eternal, the soul too is understood by many Jewish thinkers to be eternal. There is even a place where souls reside in Judaism after one has died, called *Olam HaBa* – the World to Come. Jewish teachings on the afterlife are relatively sparse. The Torah, the Five Books of Moses, has no clear reference to the afterlife at all. It has been conjectured that the silence of the Torah in this regard is due to ensure that Judaism does not evolve in the direction of the Egyptians, who were obsessed with death and mummification of its great leaders.

Since nobody has ever gone to the World to Come and returned, everything written about what happens in it is purely a matter of faith and speculation. The Talmud (Berachot 17a) describes the World to Come as a place where "there will be no eating, no drinking, or procreation or business. There will be no jealousy or hatred or competition, but the righteous will sit with crowns on their heads feasting on the radiance of the divine presence."

Despite Talmudic Judaism's assertion of a future world, polls about

Americans' religious beliefs have discovered that a far smaller percentage of Jews than Christians believe in an afterlife.

Jewish mystics explain that all living beings – human and natural – have souls. However, they also posit that all souls are not created equal, and human beings have both a *nefesh* and a *neshamah*. The *nefesh* is considered the animal soul – the life force with animalistic drives. The *neshamah* is a purely spiritual component, a divine spark which separates man from animal. This is the part that yearns for spirituality. Mystics also believe that there exists in humans a divine spiritual soul which has the ability to create a relationship with the Divine, allowing them to make moral decisions based on free will. It is this divine soul that lives on eternally, and which animals, according to them, do not possess.

There is also a Kabbalistic view of reincarnation, whereby a person's soul returns again and again in different bodies, and the way in which it conducts itself in each reincarnation determines its ascent or descent in its next visit.

Others believe that our immortality and eternal life occur biologically through the children that we bring into the world. Some understand immortality through influence, meaning that when we influence others and have them use us as role models, this kind of eternal significance is itself a form of immortality.

Although there is no consistent view on whether animals have souls, especially pets such as dogs or cats, I have given this question much thought. Over the years my pets have given me love, companionship, a less stressed life, and more days with a smile on my face. So I cannot say for sure that animals have souls, but those that I have had as pets sure have had them. All of my dogs have been uplifting to have as loving companions, and have been the light of my life. As Proverbs 20:27 reminds us: The soul is God's candle. My dogs have been my light!

2. *Can I recite the Mourner's Kaddish for my dog?*

Pet owners grow very attached to their animals. The longer they live the more attached they become – loving, beloved, trusting parts of a family. Our family (and my children who have two pugs) always acknowledge each other's pet's birthdays by sending E-Greeting cards. The death of a pet can be traumatic in someone's life, an event that is surely in need of ritual to mark it and assist mourners in moving on. When a pet dies there should be some way to commemorate them, and in Judaism, the Mourner's Kaddish is the prayer that we use when losing a loved one (human, that is). Judaism, traditionally, has no such ritual for a pet.

As we have pointed out earlier in this book, there is a distinction between pets and people. They are simply not in the same category, with humans having a higher status than animals. It therefore seems to me that it is important to distinguish people from pets, and that one ought not to enter into the very same rituals of mourning for a pet as one does for a human. So what might be an appropriate ritual?

I have seen family and friends gather after the loss of a pet and talk among themselves about its life. A candle in one's home could be lit and burned in memory of the deceased pet. In our home we have framed a picture of our deceased golden retriever and our pet doctor gave us a framed paw print of our beautiful dog after it was put to sleep, in addition to making a donation to a pet shelter in her memory.

As for saying the Mourner's Kaddish, it would seem to me that the majority of my rabbinic colleagues from all of the major branches of Judaism would not encourage the recitation of the Mourner's Kaddish to be said for a pet. On the other hand, contemporary Jews have developed some suitable rituals and prayers to help families cope with the loss of a beloved animal. There are some rabbis that have actually performed pet funerals, drawing from the Book of Psalms and reading family poems written about their pets. There is a lovely prayer from the series *Kol Haneshama: Shabbat Eve* by Rabbi David A. Teutsch. The prayer says in part: "Pour upon us your life, lift us up in our sorrow, and keep us on the path of companionship and loyalty that our animals have taught us."

Some rabbis have written prayers specifically designated for the loss of a beloved pet. In the book *Talking to God* by Naomi Levy (p. 67), there is a moving prayer that is directed to a pet. In it, it reflects the thankfulness for the friendship and companionship that the pet offered in happier times, and how much the pet will be missed but forever remembered. The prayer ends with the petition that God bless the pet.

To sum up: The sadness and grief caused by the death of one's pet is real, and the pain of those mourning a pet is genuine and authentic. But rather than reciting the traditional Mourner's Kaddish for people, my advice would be to use some of the suggested rituals in this answer, praying for God's comfort, and appropriately giving thanks for the life of the pet and for its companionship.

3. *Can I sit shiva for my pet?*

In case the reader is not familiar with the term *shiva*, it refers to the seven day period of mourning of people. It begins when the deceased is buried, and then usually lasts for seven days. Mourners are required to stay in their homes during which family and friends and members of the community will visit to formally express their condolences. Very often there will be a prayer service that will assemble in the house of *shiva* allowing the mourner to recite the Mourner's Kaddish.

Sitting an official *shiva* for a pet would obligate one's friends and community to pay condolence calls. It is important not to blur the distinction between humans and animals. And even though the loss of a pet may take time to assuage, there are better ways to mourn and seek comfort after the loss. One surely would be permitted to gather with one's family and invite close friends to spend some time sharing memories of one's pet. Lighting a candle in one's pet's memory would seem to me appropriate, and even choosing to read some Psalms or poems of comfort might also be helpful to the bereaved. Making a donation to an animal shelter in the pet's memory is a form of *tzedakah*, righteous giving, and is a fitting way to remember a pet. There are websites that one can consult on coping with the loss of a pet. Particularly helpful is The Humane Society.

Finally, CLAL, the National Jewish Center for Learning and Leadership, has created a blessing for a pet memorial service:

> "*Baruch atah she'lo chisar b'olamo davar.*"
> Blessed are You in whose world nothing is lacking.

It is filled with wonderful animals that bring joy and companionship to human beings.

4. *I've heard of Bark Mitzvahs for dogs. Can you tell me what this is all about?*

When I first heard of the Bark Mitzvah, I was somewhat in disbelief. I searched on the Internet which turned up a plethora of photos of dogs having so-called Bark Mitzvah parties in homes, catering halls, and the like. There were even invitations to ceremonies from synagogues across the country.

Recently I was in a Judaica store in Manhattan that was selling what looked like a prayer shawl for dogs. Although there were no ritual fringes on the shawl, it clearly was meant to replicate the *tallit* worn by Jewish adults. So why is it that the distinction between humans and pets when it comes to Jewish ritual continues to be blurred? People often do not think of the consequences of their actions, and there are often economic opportunities for crazes that can be sold to the public. Or people often look for yet another excuse to have a party,

Becoming a Bar or Bat Mitzvah is a spiritual transitional time in the life of a child when he or she assumes Jewish adult responsibility. It means accepting obligations and the opportunity to consciously choose to do them. Of course, animals are not able to process this kind of information.

Having never attended a Bark Mitzvah, I admittedly have no first-hand information in terms of what is entailed and what actually happens at one. I have read that some people celebrate Bark Mitzvahs for Purim entertainment, some to raise money for an animal's charity, and others just for the fun of it. I read that a Reform synagogue in Florida holds Bark Mitzvah celebrations for its congregation's dogs on Purim. Since Purim is a holiday that involves more frivolity this begins to make a little more sense. The ceremony takes place in the synagogue parking lot and not in the sanctuary. I would say that as long as there is no desecration of a holy or ritual object such as requiring a dog to wear a dog-size yarmulke or a *tallit*, and if the occasion benefits others, then it would be okay to carry forward the celebration. It would not be at all appropriate to have the Bark Mitzvah in a synagogue sanctuary, since this is a holy space for people, not animals.

In general, I would recommend pet owners try to stay away from staging events for their pets that replicate Jewish lifecycle events for humans. So even though I've read of a rabbi who performed a marriage ceremony for two myna birds, such ceremonies ought to be avoided since they trivialize the sanctity of marriage, which in Hebrew is called *kedushin*, meaning "sanctification."

5. *Is there a Jewish view of the afterlife for an animal?*

Before answering your question, some background to the Jewish afterlife. Judaism regards death as an inevitable part of life. Just as we are born, so we must die. However, there are rabbinic views of the afterlife. The expression *olam haba* (the future world) is frequently used in Talmudic literature to signify a new order of things. It has been described as a place where there is no need for eating, conducting business, nor is there any hatred or competition. Rather, righteous people sit with their crowns on their heads and enjoy the brilliance of the Divine. (Talmud, Berachot 17a)

All references to the future world and souls going there refer to humans, not animals. That being said, there is an idea in mystical Judaism that a soul of a person who dies can enter another living entity after the death of its body. In Hebrew, the technical term for this idea is *gilgul neshamot*, literally the rolling of souls. In English, three different terms are used: reincarnation, transmigration of souls, and metempsychosis. By the twelfth century the ideas of transmigration of souls appear to be taken for granted.

Those who embrace reincarnation posit that souls have an independent life, existing before and after the death of the body. The soul, they say, joins the body at an appropriate time, remains with it for a specified period, then takes leave of the body about the time of death, ready to assume its next assignment in the physical world.

Now here is where we get to the answer to your question. Mystics also used reincarnation to explain odd or unusual occurrences of human characteristics. They asked, for example, why some individuals act like animals. The answer offered is that these people carry the soul of a beast. Or why do some people act like angels. They may answer that these people carry the soul of an angelic animal, such as a sweet-mannered dog. Whereas some Kabbalists believed reincarnation applied exclusively to humans, others held that it also included animals.

Outside of the circle dedicated to the mystics, a belief in reincarnation is not widespread among the Jewish appeal. Is it true and can it happen? Does it occur? Only those who believe in the reincarnation of souls can answer with conviction.

6. *What is the proper Jewish response to the loss of your friend's pet?*

Having lost many pets over my lifetime I know firsthand how it feels to lose and have to say goodbye to a living companion. My grief (and my family's grief) often lingers for days and sometimes even months. With my children now grown and out of the house, my dog is my daily companion, always there to greet me. When I lost my last golden retriever four years ago, there was that feeling of loneliness when I walked into the house with no one to greet me. After several months I could not bear the pain of an empty house anymore, and we now have our current dog, another golden retriever with a heart of gold.

When my last golden retriever was put to sleep I received a lovely condolence note from our veterinarian, who also made a donation to an animal charity in her memory. It was comforting to receive words of comfort from her caregiver, and I would highly recommend reaching out to your friend to express personal condolences in addition to considering writing a note of condolence as well. In your note you will want to acknowledge the loss of your friend's pet and how you felt upon hearing the news. Let your friend know your sadness so that your friend will be reminded that he is not alone in his suffering. If you can recall a memory about your friend's dog that would also likely be most appreciated.

Since it is Jewish custom to make a charitable contribution in memory of our loved ones, I think you may also want to consider a charitable contribution as a way of showing your support to your friend and in addition doing some good for other animals. (You can review some of the animal charities that are listed in Part 1 of this book.)

The Hebrew words *baruch dayan ha'emet*, meaning Praised is the True Judge are reflexively uttered by many Jews (who are of course familiar with the custom) in response to human death and tragedy. I have no objection to saying them upon the loss of a pet as well. There are some Jewish legal authorities that would agree with me. Others find precedence for doing so, but only in the context of financial loss. That is to say, if an animal is a source of one's income (such as a breeder) or a blind person reciting the blessing upon the passing of his guide dog, since such dogs are difficult to replace.

According to the ancient sages, the mitzvah of offering comfort to the bereaved is one of the great ones. Anything that you can do to show your support for your friend's loss and help assuage his pain would be the right thing to do.

7. *I am to be married very soon. Is it okay to include my cat in my wedding ceremony?*

First of all, let me wish you a hearty mazal tov and congratulations. As a congregational rabbi one of my greatest joys is officiating at wedding ceremonies. Within Jewish tradition, marriage is both a divine commandment and the ideal human state. The Bible expresses this thought in the very beginning when it refers to Adam and Eve: "And thus shall a man leave his father and mother and cling to his wife, so they shall be one flesh." (Genesis 2:14)

The Hebrew language has no precise word for marriage. The Bible refers to a man "taking a wife." However, the rabbis elevated the idea of marriage by calling it *kiddushin* – sanctification, which contains in it the word *kadosh* – holy. A Jewish marriage is more than a civil relationship. It is a sanctification, a consecration encompassing an entire way of life. Jewish weddings consecrate husband and wife to each other in a relationship of sacred trust.

Since there is an aura of profound sanctity attached to marriage by our tradition, I would be sensitive if I were you to how people would perceive your inclusion of your pet cat in your wedding ceremony. Undoubtedly some would be taken aback by having an animal under a wedding canopy, and there are even those who may be allergic to cats present at your wedding. And of course, it would not be suitable if your wedding were held in a synagogue sanctuary to have your cat there with you.

Perhaps a better idea might be to have a picture of your cat on some sort of poster at your wedding, indicating your love for your cat and giving your cat a pictorial presence. In that way you will retain the sanctity of your wedding while still giving your cat the honor of having its image there. With modern photographic technology, you could also photoshop your cat into one of your wedding pictures and hang the picture at home. That might be a nice compromise.

8. *A tragedy occurred. My aunt and her beloved cat were killed in an auto accident. Can they be buried side by side in a Jewish cemetery?*

Igniting the religious furor over the sanctity of a final resting place, the owners of a Jewish cemetery on the North Side of Chicago wanted to clear an unused corner of their property and open the city's only burial ground for pets. It outraged Jewish community leaders, who thought it would be demeaning and degrading to people to have to be buried adjacent to a pet cemetery.

The ritualized burial of animals has been practiced in virtually every part of the world at some point in time. Of all countries, Egypt is the most famous for conducting funerals and burials for its animals, beginning in the time of the ancient Pharaohs. Today in the United States there are more than five hundred pet cemeteries. Westchester County's Hartsdale Pet Cemetery, one of the oldest burial places for animals, has a chaplain who routinely holds formal funeral services for its deceased animals. He typically reads from the Book of Genesis to attendees of his Jewish pet funerals and always uses the 23rd Psalm of comfort. There are quite a number of Stars of David on the tombstones, too.

Many people today choose to bury their pets in their own backyards or have them euthanized and then cremated, often holding onto their ashes in an urn. There are rabbinic authorities that would permit either burial or cremation for one's deceased pet. I am not aware of any Jewish cemetery that allows its pet to be buried next to the remains of a human. I also feel that the money used to bury a pet in a pet cemetery would be better spent to enhance the lives of abused animals by donating to an animal charity. There are tombstones today (including in our own local Jewish cemetery) that have a picture of the deceased etched on it. One could conceivably also etch an image of one's beloved pet on the stone, or a mentioning of the pet in an engraving, which might be a way of keeping a pet close to one's heart without it actually being buried with its owner.

TOPIC 6   **Kosher Living**

1. *Is it okay to hunt animals for sport?*

Hunting is a very popular sport in the United States and other Western societies, but is not practiced very much among Jews. There are no statements in Jewish tradition and literature that speak of hunting for sport in a positive way. According to Jewish law, it is permitted to slay animals in the wild only when they invade human settlements, but to pursue them in the forest where they reside when they are not invading human areas in prohibited. There is rabbinic authority for permitting the hunting of animals for financial reasons (e.g., one who deals with skins for making clothing). Biblical law also prohibits the eating of any animal not killed instantly and with a single stroke, which would also make hunting forbidden to Jews as a method of acquiring food.

Many discussions of the morality of hunting have appeared in magazines. One writer, Joseph Wood Krutch, commented that ordinary killers "are selfish and unscrupulous, but their deeds are not gratuitously evil. The killer for sport has no such comprehensible motive. He prefers death to life, darkness to light. He gets nothing except the satisfaction of saying 'something which wanted to live is dead.'"

The deliberate shooting of an animal for no other reason than sport is not recognized as "kosher living." The great hunters in the Bible are Nimrod (Genesis 10:9) and Esau (Genesis 25:27), neither of whom was celebrated by our ancient rabbis as righteous people. The Jewish dietary laws with its system of spiritual discipline have trained the Jew each and every day to have reverence for life, even though life must be taken to provide him with food. By restricting the kinds of animals which may be eaten, and providing for a humane slaughter and a trained slaughterer, we are prevented from becoming brutalized by the killing of animals for our food.

In contrast to Jewish ritual slaughter, the death of hunted animals can often be prolonged and painful. From the perspective of Jewish law, Jews are forbidden to eat animals killed by hunting. This prohibition has become so ingrained in the Jewish psyche that even among Jewish people who have long since stopped observing the Jewish dietary laws, one finds relatively few Jews whose hobby is hunting animals for sport. Hunters risk becoming hardened and cruel through the act of destroying animal life. Better to be soft-hearted and good.

2. *Is it proper for Jews to own and wear a fur coat?*

In recent times many animal activists have strongly protested stores in the fur business. A number of parameters would render some furs kosher for wear and others forbidden. If the wearing of furs provides for a legitimate need (that is, the fur will keep a person warmer than other materials), then I suppose it would be permissible. The reality today, though, is that artificial materials would keep a person equally warm.

Many women choose to buy fur coats to display their wealth and make a fashion statement. In such a case, this would be considered frivolous and not a legitimate need. I also want to mention that even when furs are permitted, they may not be acquired from animals that were trapped and clubbed and put through tortuous pain. Using such trapped animals would be in violation of the Jewish law of unnecessarily causing pain to animals.

To this day many animals whose skins are used in furs are trapped in steel leg hold traps and suffer hours of pain. In addition, a fur coat such as mink requires the killing of dozens of animals in order to manufacture one single fur coat. At a time when fur coats can be made of synthetic materials that do not require the painful and cruel deaths of animals, the question any religious person must ask is: "Is this what God really wants of me?"

3. *What's wrong with eating veal?*

Veal meat is derived from a calf, and if slaughtered in a proper manner by a kosher slaughterer, it is entirely acceptable. But some people who call themselves eco-kosher consider eating veal to be *treif* (not kosher). This is because when calves are factory-farmed, the animals are often kept in cramped, despicable conditions. To ensure the meat's tenderness, factory-farmed calves are often immobilized in a contraption that does not permit them to graze, and they are force-fed. Consequently, so-called eco-kosher Jews will refrain from eating any kind of meat when they know that the animal from which the meat is produced is treated without true concern for its welfare. These same people are also not likely to buy vegetables treated with pesticides.

As the greening of Judaism takes root across the country, eco-kosher is just one of the many earth-friendly trends that seems to be gaining momentum. Synagogues of all denominations are now beginning to look for more ways to integrate ideas coming from the eco-kosher movement. To give one example, in our synagogue we try to use cloth table coverings instead of the disposable variety.

If you want more information about this fast-growing eco-kosher movement you can contact the Coalition on the Environment and Jewish Life.

4. *What makes an animal kosher?*

Chapter 11 of the Book of Leviticus and chapter 14 of the Book of Deuteronomy list the characteristics of a kosher animal: it must have hooves that are fully split, and it must chew its cud. If only one of these characteristics is present in the animal, it is not kosher. Thus, animals such as horses and rabbits, which chew their cud but do not have genuine split hooves, are not kosher; nor are pigs, which have split hooves but do not chew their cud. On the other hand, oxen, sheep, deer, and goats fulfill both requirements and are therefore kosher.

For meat to be considered kosher, a kosher animal must be slaughtered by a Jewish ritual slaughterer who is both skilled and possesses personal piety. The entire process demands rigid inspection. If the animal to be slaughtered is a kosher one, the hindquarters are separated from the forequarters, because the forbidden sciatic nerve is deeply imbedded in the muscle tissue of the hindquarters and can be removed only with great difficulty. For this reason hindquarters are set aside and are sold as non-kosher. That is why real sirloin or T-bone steaks are not kosher.

5. *Is it okay for me to offer my blessing to my pet on Friday nights at the Shabbat dinner table?*

It is customary for Jewish parents to bless their children before sitting down to the Sabbath meal. This provides them with a privileged opportunity to express appreciation for their children – something they may not always have the leisure to do during the busy and hectic week. Through the touch of a parent's hands or the sound of a parent's voice, children can feel and respond to the love and affection their family has for them.

The traditional blessing for boys invokes the shining examples of Jacob's grandchildren Ephraim and Manasseh, who, although raised in Egypt, did not lose their identities as Jews. The blessing for girls refers to the four matriarchs Sarah, Rebekah, Rachel, and Leah, all of whom were known for their concern and compassion for others. The brief ceremony concludes with the priestly benediction invoking God's protection and peace.

When my children were young, my wife and I so much enjoyed the opportunity of laying our hands on their heads and offering them a blessing. Now that they are grown up and no longer living in our house, the third member at our Sabbath meal is our golden retriever Lexi. We feel compelled, since she is such an integral member of our family, to offer her a prayer on Friday night. Each week Lexi has learned to lower her head as I place my hands on it and offer her the following:

> We love having you as our pet
> You light up our lives with joy.
> May God continue to watch over you
> Giving you health and peace.
> We love you

My Methodist Minister Colleague in my town has been offering blessings to the pets of her members for many years. Parishioners bring their pets on a designated Sunday to receive her prayer and blessing. Last year for the first time I, too, had an opportunity to bless the animals at our local Jewish Community Center on a Sunday afternoon which was called "Dog Day at the J." A variety of dogs (owned by Jews and non-Jews alike) came to an outdoor area at the JCC. My dog Lexi was there as well. I spoke about the importance of treating our pets with respect and dignity, and followed with this blessing:

> Blessed are You, Creator of all
> Maker of all living creatures
> On the fifth and sixth days of the creation of the world
> You brought forth the living creatures in the sea
> Birds in the skies and animals on the land.
> You inspired us to call animals brothers and sisters
> We ask you to offer your blessing of peace and love
> On all of our pets who are gathered here today
> Enable them to live in full praises to Your Name

May we continue to offer You praise
For the beauty of Your creation
Praised are You, Sovereign of the World,
In all of Your creatures. Amen.

6. *Should animals be used in medical research?*

The Bible is very clear in mandating humans to exercise their mastery over the animals of the world, as set forth in the story of Adam and Eve. Animals are meant to serve humankind, but must be treated with compassion and respect. The specific permission to use animals for medical experimentation despite their potential sufferings was made famous in the Code of Jewish Law (Even Ha-ezer 5:15): "Whatever is needed for medicinal purposes or for other things does not entail a violation of the prohibition of prevention of the cruelty to animals." This ruling is exceedingly broad, allowing for future needs that even the Code of Law could not have imagined. Later rabbinic commentators attempted to define the area of medical research in greater detail. For example, it was deemed that substantial need would be a criterion, not just scientific whimsy in order to justify experimentation with animals. Exactly what constitutes substantial need is still fodder for debate, and so there is no clearly defined single Jewish view of medical experimentation on animals.

In his *Encyclopedia of Jewish Medical Ethics* (vol. 1, p. 264), Dr. Avraham Steinberg attempts to catalogue all of the preferred practices that over the years have been proposed: there must be *bona fide* need, one must engage in the least possible number of experiments, all efforts to reduce the animal's suffering must be taken into account, lower life forms for experimentation are always to be preferred, and when the experiment is finished, any animal lingering in pain should be euthanized.

The prevailing view today on this issue asserts that the pain of the animal surely counts less than the pain of sick people who might be helped by such research. This appears to be the prevailing opinion, provided of course that all reasonable steps are taken to prevent any unnecessary suffering and to limit the practice strictly to the advancement of human health.

7. *Is it okay to race horses and is there a Jewish view on watching horse races?*

The ancient Sages strictly forbid any participation in spectacles in which animals are pitted against humans or against other animals. The gladiatorial battles of Roman times, including those that matched human fighters against animals, were abhorrent to our ancient sages. Today, in our time, cockfights, bullfights, dogfights, and other similar activities are forbidden as a violation of the law that prevents cruelty to animals.

But do these prohibitions also apply to horse races? There are sages who allow watching horse races in order to learn the proper art of riding and to learn how to judge the quality of horse that one might want to buy. To the extent that these competitions are tests of skill, Jewish law can be understood to permit Jews who own horses to race their own animals as well as watch other horses run in races. If, however, these races lead to intentional injury of either animals or their riders, then they would be considered prohibited. In our own modern day, the strict rules and regulations of horse racing are supposed to guarantee that both horse and rider are protected from abuse and injury.

Judaism also has a view of gambling, and compulsive gambling on horse racing was frowned upon. Occasional gambling though would be permitted, and all the more so when the winnings would be given to a charitable cause.

8. *Is there a Jewish viewpoint concerning visiting a zoo or aquarium?*

I love to visit zoos, and often went with my children when they were young at least once or twice a year. I also enjoyed visiting aquariums and seeing the array and beauty of aquatic life. Because animals and fish are God's creations and part of God's world, we are allowed to share in their beauty by visiting them up close and learning how they live and what they look like. There are many stories of famous rabbis who enjoyed visiting zoos, and on the intermediate days of Passover when I would often have time to visit the Bronx zoo, hundreds of Orthodox Jews were there with their large families, munching on matzah while standing and watching in awe the many animals that are housed there.

There are actually some positives from a Jewish perspective when visiting a zoo or an aquarium. One is that many of these places help preserve some of the more rare and endangered species. Secondly, because Judaism so highly values learning, visiting a zoo presents an opportunity to learn more about these creatures. There is a wonderful biblical zoo in Jerusalem which I have visited that provides information on its signs so that the visitor learns where and in what book of the Bible a particular animal is mentioned.

Finally, visiting a zoo presents the Jewish visitor with the opportunity to recite the special blessing that one says in order to thank God for having created such a variety of creatures in this world:

Praised are You, Sovereign of the World, who creates a variety of living creatures.
Baruch ata Adonai Eloheinu melech ha'olam meshanneh ha-briyot.

You may want to visit the website of a contemporary Orthodox Rabbi, Natan Slifkin, which affords its visitors a chance to learn more about animal creatures and their connection to the Torah. The site is www .zootorah.com.

9. *Are there any ethical considerations when buying kosher meat or fish of which I should be aware?*

While the thrust of biblical and Talmudic law is to reduce animal suffering, there are indeed some food items that are widely regarded as kosher, but which should be forbidden for consumption by both Jews and non-Jews alike.

The first is veal, which comes from a kosher animal, but whose treatment is questionable to say the least. Ten years ago newborn calves were being raised in semi-dark narrow wooden crates and fed on diets very low in iron so that the calf's flesh will retain the pale pink color and soft texture of prime veal. These calves were also denied hay and straw for bedding. Such treatment of a kosher animal violates both the letter and spirit of the law. Unless these conditions improve, it seems to me that we should continue to refrain from eating veal in order to send a message to the farmers who raise the veal calves.

Foie gras refers to the fattened liver of geese and ducks, two birds which are considered kosher. Regretfully, the fattened livers do not come naturally. Rather, the birds are force-fed until their livers grow eight times their normal size. The geese are generally kept in extremely small pens and fed by means of a metal tube that is inserted into their throats. As is the case with veal, such cruelty to animals is allowed because some people enjoy a certain taste.

Finally, there are some specific problems in the fishing industry. Dolphins, non-kosher aquatic mammals often swim above schools of tuna (a kosher fish). When fishermen cast their nets for tuna, dolphins are frequently caught in the nets and often killed in the process. Certainly if dolphins are mixed with tuna in the catch and not removed, the mixture is not kosher. But our concern ought to be with the dolphins who are often needlessly killed. Given the fact that we can find dolphin-safe marked tuna for sale, we should look for this tuna when shopping.

10. *My dog had a litter of five puppies. Nobody wants them and I do not have room for them. What is the right thing to do with them?*

There are lots of families whose dogs end up giving birth to large litters and have no idea how to care for them. That is why we are in favor of spaying our animals so that we can control the pet population and avoid predicaments such as yours. That being said, the first thing I would do is to see whether there are any people you know and trust that might be willing to take one of your litter to keep and raise as a pet. Your next step would be to look for a reputable animal shelter that would accept the puppies for adoption. You might also want to speak to your veterinarian for his or her ideas. Generally pet doctors have lots of contacts.

11. *Why is there a restriction requirement to drain blood from an animal before eating it?*

The ban on eating blood is the most basic eating rule in the Five Books of Moses. First, an animal that dies naturally or at the hands of another beast may not be eaten, for its blood cannot be properly removed. Second, the blood of sacrificial animals must be collected for purification rites or drained beside the altar. Third, the blood of an animal that is slaughtered must be returned to God.

Regarding the eating of kosher meat, all kosher meat must be drained of blood in the slaughtering house and then soaked and salted after butchering. When I was a child my mother would also broil our liver. I never knew the reason why. I now realize that in broiling the liver all of the blood is drained, which fulfills the kosher law.

It is not enough in Judaism that the animal must be killed in a most humane way. Going further, even the symbol of life, the blood itself, must be removed. As Deuteronomy 12:23 reminds us: "Be steadfast in not eating the blood; for the blood is the life, and you shall not eat the blood with the flesh." There is no clearer visible symbol of life than blood. To spill blood is to bring death. To inject blood is often to save a life, a mitzvah in Judaism. The removal of blood which the Jewish dietary laws require is one of the most powerful means of making people constantly aware of the concession and compromise which the whole act of eating meat, in reality, is. Again, it teaches us reverence for life.

12. *Why are Jewish people forbidden to eat the hind part of a cow?*

According to Genesis 32:32, it is forbidden to eat the sciatic nerve of cattle and sheep. The custom commemorates the struggle of Jacob and the angel, and Jacob's injury. It is necessary, therefore, for the Jewish ritual slaughterer to remove the sciatic nerve, a procedure which involves skillful hands. Ashkenazic rabbinic authorities have decided that we are not sufficiently expert in removing the sciatic nerve and that kosher homes and restaurants may not serve meat from the hindquarters (containing T-bone and sirloin steaks). In Sephardic communities, however, and in Israel, there are specially trained people who have expertise in the removal of veins and nerves, and thus it is possible to get kosher meat from the hindquarters.

Dr. Ed Greenstein, in his commentary on the Jewish Dietary Laws in the Etz Hayim Torah and Commentary (p. 1460), has an interesting explanation and a rationale for not eating the hindquarter. He posits that because all of Jacob's immediate descendants are called literally "those issuing from his thigh," the ban is meant to draw attention to the ongoing condition of Israel as a people impaired but managing to survive. The impaired thigh tendon signifies the people of Israel, and because of that symbolism, the Israelites and all of their descendants are not to eat the part of the animal with which they are taught to identify themselves. In other words, the eating rule is to remind the Jews of who they are and from whom they are descended.

One of my favorite television commercials is the Hebrew National kosher hot dog one, which says that "we appeal answer to a higher authority." They then show a picture of a cow divided into parts, saying: "No ifs, ands, or butts."

13. *Are there any times of the year when Jews are forbidden to eat meat?*

The days between the seventeenth of Tammuz and the ninth of Av (in the summer) are considered days of mourning, in which the Jewish people commemorate the collapse of the Jerusalem Temple. Weddings and other joyous celebrations do not take place during this period. A further element of mourning is added during the "nine days" between the first and the ninth of Av. During this period the pious refrain from eating meat and drinking wine, except on the Sabbath on which it is forbidden to mourn.

14. *I keep kosher and I once heard that giraffe is a kosher animal. Is this really true?*

The Torah states that all kosher animals need to have split hooves and chew their cud. The giraffe is not only the tallest cud chewer but also has split hooves. Thus, it does indeed fit the category of kosher. In fact, many Torah commentaries identify the animal called a zemer (Deuteronomy 14:4) as the giraffe.

It is a myth to think that Jews who keep kosher do not eat giraffe because of its neck. (i.e., the ritual slaughterer would not know exactly where to make the cut). This is not true, since there are Talmudic passages that present the precise measurements for where to cut the neck. The real legal basis for not eating giraffe is because Jewish communities and their rabbinic representatives generally require a continuous tradition of eating the specific animal in question. Since there is no continuous tradition for eating giraffe, you will not find it on a kosher restaurant menu.